SMALL *Oxford* BOOKS

GARDENS & GARDENERS

SMALL *Oxford* BOOKS

GARDENS & GARDENERS

Compiled by
ELIZABETH SEAGER

Oxford New York
OXFORD UNIVERSITY PRESS
1984

Oxford University Press, Walton Street, Oxford OX2 6DP

*London Glasgow New York Toronto
Delhi Bombay Calcutta Madras Karachi
Kuala Lumpur Singapore Hong Kong Tokyo
Nairobi Dar es Salaam Cape Town
Melbourne Auckland
and associated companies in*

Beirut Berlin Ibadan Mexico City Nicosia

Oxford is a trade mark of Oxford University Press

*Compilation, introduction, and editorial matter
© Elizabeth Seager 1984*

*All rights reserved. No part of this publication may be reproduced,
stored in a retrieval system, or transmitted, in any form or by any means,
electronic, mechanical, photocopying, recording, or otherwise, without
the prior permission of Oxford University Press*

British Library Cataloguing in Publication Data
Seager, Elizabeth
Gardens and gardeners.—(Small Oxford books)
1. Gardens—Literary collections
2. English literature
I. Title
820'.8'036 PR1111.G3
ISBN 0-19-214151-1

Library of Congress Cataloging in Publication Data
Main entry under title:
Gardens & gardeners.
(Small Oxford books)
Includes index.
1. Gardens—Addresses, essays, lectures. 2. Gardens
—Literary collections. 3. Gardeners—Addresses,
essays, lectures. 4. Gardeners—Literary collections.
5. Gardening—Addresses, essays, lectures. 6. Gardening
—Literary collections. I. Seager, Elizabeth.
II. Title: Gardens and gardeners.
SB455.G36 1984   635   83-19465
ISBN 0-19-214151-1

✻

For my mother,

who inspired my interest

in plants and gardens

*Set by New Western Printing Ltd.
Printed in Great Britain by
Hazell Watson & Viney Limited
Aylesbury, Bucks*

Introduction

When adolescence is passed the mind becomes, to a great extent, settled, and one acquires a bit of land of one's own. That is the beginning of your real gardener, and it is then that gardeners are made.

H. L. V. Fletcher, *Purest Pleasure*, 1948

Just after my marriage almost twenty-five years ago, there arrived through the post a damp packet labelled, to my husband's mystification, *Old Man by the Back Door*. Unwrapped, this was found to contain a cutting of *Artemisia abrotanum* – commonly known by such contradictory names as old man, lad's love, maid's ruin, and southernwood – taken by my mother from the bush that grew by the back door of my childhood home. Carefully planted in our new garden it thrived and grew into a large aromatic shrub, from which cuttings were eventually brought to our present garden.

From then on I was hooked, and gardening catalogues became – and still are – favourite bedtime reading. Soon the botanical Latin names of plants were as familiar to me as their common names, and as a remedy for insomnia I still find nothing better than reciting them alphabetically – *Azara, Ballota, Coronilla, Daphne* – an incantation soothing enough to induce sleep long before the trickier Qs and Xs are reached.

Never mind if that first garden was tiny, I could still dream, and there are fewer daydreams more satisfying than a gardener's. Household chores whizz past when you are mentally shifting all the shrubs in your garden to accommodate some longed-for treasure.

My own methods of gardening are random, and as our cottage is set, in traditional manner, at the back of its plot, the complete garden is revealed at once to the passer-by: a patchwork of vegetables, fruit and flowers. Rhubarb unfurls under the rambler roses; poppies, peonies, fennel and fuchsia jostle clematis and catmint beneath old plum, lilac, and apple trees, while self-sown foxgloves and sweet rocket grow as they please. Being uncompetitive by temperament I grow nothing for show, and garden solely for my own pleasure, using no weedkillers, but hand-weeding instead for relaxation and enjoyment.

The nineteenth-century gardening cleric Canon Ellacombe commented that his Gloucestershire garden was full of forget-me-nots – not just the small blue *Myosotis*, but many plants of all kinds that reminded him of friends and places from which they came. Our plot is full of similar forget-me-nots, and though a few shrubs have been bought to mark anniversaries, most have been grown from cuttings, reminding me of happy times or favourite places.

Pottering in our garden, surrounded by its wildlife and accompanied by Sophie the cat – or sitting there with my husband to enjoy its scents, sights, and sounds – I experience a satisfying sense of continuity in enjoying the same small pleasures that have delighted generations of gardeners; in growing some of the plants they knew; in using basic tools that have changed little over the centuries, and in voicing age-old grumbles about weather, weeds, or pests.

When visiting famous gardens I can appreciate the landscaped splendour of Cliveden or Rousham, and admire the breadth of vision shown by their creators – but it is the plant-packed intimacy of Hidcote or Trelissick that excites and delights me. Ordinary gardens too, glimpsed through gateways or over walls are a source of unending pleasure – a tiny terrace plot magnificent in May with just one enormous tree peony, crown imperials in regal superiority outside a village store, or a sunny cottage window crowded with cacti. I hope that the gardens and gardeners – ancient and modern – glimpsed in the following pages will provide as much enjoyment.   E.A.S.

The use of gardens... as it has been the inclination of kings and the choice of philosophers, so it has been the common favourite of public and private men; a pleasure of the greatest and the care of the meanest; and indeed an employment and a possession for which no man is too high or too low.

Sir William Temple, *Upon the Gardens of Epicurus*,
1685

Gardeners

The dictionary defines a gardener as 'one who gardens, or is skilled in gardening'. In common usage the word carries overtones of competence, knowledge, or flair. However, by no means all who garden are green-fingered, and though most of us enjoy our gardening, be it casually or passionately, there are others who plod away resentfully or ignorantly. Biblical tradition presents Adam as the first gardener. Whether or not he enjoyed his occupation is unknown, though he certainly had little choice in the matter.

And the Lord God planted a garden eastward in Eden; and there he put the man whom he had formed.

And out of the ground made the Lord God to grow every tree that is pleasant to the sight, and good for food; the tree of life also in the midst of the garden, and the tree of knowledge of good and evil.

And the Lord God took the man, and put him into the garden of Eden to dress it and keep it.

Genesis 2: 8, 9, 15

Karel Čapek, the Czech playwright, had a rebellious attitude towards gardening when he was a child because, like Adam, he was forbidden to pick the unripe fruit in his father's garden. In later life gardening became his passion. He grew alpines, orchids, and cacti in his Prague town garden, and produced a humorous, perceptive best-seller on gardening.

While one is in the prime of youth one thinks that a flower is what one carries in a buttonhole, or presents to a girl; one somehow does not rightly understand that a flower is something which hibernates, which is dug round and manured, watered and transplanted, divided and trimmed, tied up, freed from weeds, and cleaned of seeds, dead leaves, aphis and mildew; instead of digging the garden one runs after girls, satisfies one's ambition, eats the fruit of life which one has not produced oneself, and, on the whole, behaves destructively. A certain maturity, or let us say paternity, is necessary for a man to become an amateur gardener. Besides, you must have your own garden. Usually you have it laid out by an expert, and you think that you will go and look at it when the day's work is over, and enjoy the flowers, and listen to the chirping of the birds. One day you may plant one little flower with your own hand; I planted a house-leek. Perhaps a bit of soil will get into your body through the quick, or in some other way, and cause blood-poisoning or inflammation. One claw and the whole bird is caught. Another time you may catch it from your neighbours; you see that a campion is flowering in your neighbour's garden, and you say: 'By Jove! Why shouldn't it grow in mine as well? I'm blessed if I can't do better than that'.

From such beginnings the gardener yields more and more to this newly awakened passion, which is nourished by repeated success and spurred on by each new failure; the passion of the collector bursts out in him, driving him to raise everything according to the alphabet from *Acaena* to *Zauschneria*; then a craze for specialization breaks out in him, which makes of a hitherto normal being a rose- dahlia- or some other sort of exalted maniac. Others fall victims to an artistic passion, and continually alter and rearrange their beds, devise colour schemes, move shrubs, and change whatever stands or grows, urged on by a creative discontent. Let no one think that real gardening is a bucolic and meditative occupation. It is an insatiable passion, like everything else to which a man gives his heart.

Karel Čapek, *The Gardener's Year*, 1929

GARDENERS

Garden and Terrace, Montacute, Somerset

Another addict in Kent:

I began to set out the Oval Garden at Say[e]s Court, which was before a rude orchard, and all the rest one entire field of 100 acres, without any hedge: excepting the hither holly-hedge joining to the bank of the mount walk: and this was the beginning of all the succeeding gardens, walks, groves, enclosures and plantations there...

John Evelyn, *Diary*, 17 January 1653

Is it not possible for your Excellency to bring over some of those quince and cherry-trees, which your Lordship so celebrates? I suppose they might be secured in barrels or packed up, as they transport other rarities from far countries.

John Evelyn, letter to the Earl of Sandwich, Britain's Ambassador at Madrid, 21 August 1668

Sayes-Court quickly became famous and its visitors included the foremost personalities of the day. There, two great diarists walked and talked together.

Then to Mr Evelyn's... he showed me his gardens, which are, for variety of evergreens, and hedge of holly, the finest things I ever saw in my life. Thence in his coach to Greenwich, and there to my office, all the way having fine discourse of trees and the nature of vegetables.

Samuel Pepys, *Diary*, 5 October 1665

Another writer, Chekhov, was an enthusiastic gardener on his Russian estate of Melikhovo. As befits the author of The Cherry Orchard *he*

bought young trees in quantity: fifty cherries, a hundred lilacs, eighty apples; some were destroyed by hares, but restocking proceeded apace. He also asked his sister to bring seeds of fir, pine, larch and oak from Moscow, and cultivated these. He lopped dead branches, felled dead trees, developed muscles suitable for a circus strong man. Pruning roses was also among his skills, and he planted tulips, lilies, daffodils, hyacinths and irises in quantity.

Ronald Hingley, *A New Life of Chekhov*, 1976

Flowering trees were also the delight of an earlier gardener, Po-Chü-i, a provincial Governor of Chung-Chou in ninth-century China.

I took money and bought flowering trees
And planted them out on the bank to the east of the Keep.
I simply bought whatever had most blooms,
Not caring whether peach, apricot, or plum.
A hundred fruits, all mixed up together;
A thousand branches, flowering in due rotation.
Each has its season coming early or late;
But to all alike the fertile soil is kind.
The red flowers hang like a heavy mist;
The white flowers gleam like a fall of snow.
The wandering bees cannot bear to leave them;
The sweet birds also come there to roost.
In front there flows an ever-running stream;
Beneath there is built a little flat terrace.

GARDENERS

Sometimes I sweep the flagstones of the terrace;
Sometimes, in the wind, I raise my cup and drink.
The flower-branches screen my head from the sun;
The flower-buds fall down into my lap.
Alone drinking, alone singing my songs,
I do not notice that the moon is level with the steps.
The people of Pa do not care for flowers;
All the spring no one has come to look.
But their Governor-General, alone with his cup of wine,
Sits in the evening and will not move from the place!

> Po-Chü-i, trans. Arthur Waley, 170 *Chinese Poems*, 1920

Planning a garden can be even more enjoyable than the finished result:

Half the interest of a garden is the constant exercise of the imagination. You are always living three, or indeed six, months hence. I believe that people entirely devoid of imagination never can be really good gardeners. To be content with the present, and not striving about the future, is fatal.

> Mrs C. W. Earle, *Pot-Pourri from a Surrey Garden*, 1897

I enjoy our garden in my mind. I have been in it, thought about it, planned for it so often and so long that I know it far better than the proverbial back of my hand. I must look at my hand to remember its contours. But the garden is there in my mind's eye – each tree, each stump or exposed root, each bank or slope or wall, each clump of flowers or peppering of bulbs. Travelling in the train or lying awake at night, I can savour the garden, plan the next improvement, pass my mind over its textures as if I were passing my hand.

> Michael Dower, 'Living with a Garden', from *The Countryman*, Summer 1974

The man or the woman who possesses a gift for creating beautiful daydream gardens is to be envied. It is a joy that never fails. Maybe the possessor of it does not own a garden, or if he does it is so small that none of the weavings of imagination can take shape in it. Yet wherever the dreamer goes he will be happy. If he is not actually building castles in the air, he will be noting certain colour-combinations, effects of light and shade, happy homes for flowers, shape and line in architecture or in natural hills and dales, which may some day be adapted to his friend's garden, if not to his own.

Viscountess Wolseley, Gardens, their Form and Design, 1919

A dream that became reality at Sissinghurst in Kent:

For my own part, I am trying to make a grey, green, and white garden. This is an experiment which I ardently hope may be successful, though I doubt it. One's best ideas seldom play up in practice to one's expectations, especially in gardening, where everything looks so well on paper and in the catalogues, but fails so lamentably in fulfilment after you have tucked your plants into the soil. Still, one hopes.

My grey, green and white garden will have the advantage of a high yew hedge behind it, a wall along one side, a strip of box edging along another side, and a path of old brick along a fourth side. It is, in fact, nothing more than a fairly large bed, which has now been divided into halves by a short path of grey flagstones terminating in a rough wooden seat. When you sit on this seat, you will be turning your backs to the yew hedge, and from there I hope you will survey a low sea of grey clumps of foliage, pierced here and there with tall white flowers. I visualize the white trumpets of dozens of regale lilies, grown three years ago from seed, coming up through the grey of southernwood and artemisia and cotton-lavender, with grey-and-white edging plants such as *Dianthus* 'Mrs Sinkins' and the silvery mats of *Stachys lanata*, more familiar and so much nicer under its English names of rabbit's ears or saviour's flannel. There will be white pansies, and white peonies, and white irises with their grey leaves ... at least, I hope there will be all these things. I don't want to boast in advance about my grey, green, and white garden. It may be a terrible failure. I wanted only to suggest that such experiments are worth trying, and that you can adapt them to your own taste and your own opportunities.

All the same, I cannot help hoping that the great ghostly barn-owl will sweep silently across a pale garden, next summer, in the twilight – the pale garden that I am now planting, under the first flakes of snow.

V. Sackville-West, *In Your Garden*, 1951

In Victorian Pomerania, rigid social convention dictated that upper-class women did not actually garden themselves, and for the young English Countess von Arnim, who wrote under the pseudonym 'Elizabeth', this led to frustrations. At Nassenheide, her husband's country estate, the Countess strove to introduce an English informality in the face of opposition from unimaginative gardeners.

I am ignorant, and the gardener is, I do believe, still more so; for he was forcing some tulips, and they have all shrivelled up and died, and he says that he cannot imagine why. Besides, he is in love with the cook, and is going to marry her after Christmas, and refuses to enter into any of my plans with the enthusiasm they deserve, but sits with vacant eye dreamily chopping wood from morning till night to keep the beloved one's kitchen fire well supplied. I cannot understand anyone preferring cooks to marigolds; those future marigolds, shadowy as they are, and whose seeds are still sleeping at the seedsman's, have shone through my winter days like golden lamps.

I wish with all my heart I were a man, for of course the first thing I should do would be to buy a spade and go and garden, and then I should have the delight of doing everything for my flowers with my own hands and need not waste time explaining what I want done to somebody else. It is dull work giving orders and trying to describe the bright visions of one's brain to a person who has no visions and no brain, and who thinks a yellow bed should be calceolarias edged with blue.

Countess von Arnim, *Elizabeth and Her German Garden*, 1898

Five years later in England, Lady Wolseley took the then unconventional step of employing a female gardener, an event which was to inspire her daughter Frances, later Viscountess Wolseley, to create one of the first colleges for lady gardeners.

The applicant for the gardener's place dined here and slept here while I was away. Frances was much struck by her. An *absolute* lady, *and* didn't flinch at manure stirring, or scullery drain, or anything! An unhappy marriage, and failing in market gardening has brought her to this. Dean Hole most strongly recommends her, and has known her all his life. She says, 'I think I have forty years' work still in me.' Poor lady, at eighty-two she will begin digging her own grave perhaps.

Lady Wolseley, letter to her husband, 22 February 1903

GARDENERS

In the early nineteenth century it was unusual for a woman to stray outside the flower garden:

I saw, on the 7th of November last, a very pretty woman, in the village of Hannington, in Wiltshire, digging a piece of ground and planting it with early cabbages, which she did as handily and as neatly as any gardener that ever I saw. The ground was wet, and therefore, to avoid treading the digged ground in that state, she had her line extended, and put in the rows as she advanced in her digging, standing in the trench while she performed the act of planting, which she did with great nimbleness and precision. Nothing could be more skilfully or beautifully done. Her clothes were neat, clean, and tight about her.

William Cobbett, Cottage Economy, 1822

Later that century the middle-class lady pottering among her flowers was advised to wear

a gardening apron, composed of stout Holland, with ample pockets to contain her pruning-knife, a small stout hammer, a bale of string, and a few nails and snippings of cloth.

The second article which I pronounce to be indispensable is a pair of Indian rubber shoes, or the wooden high-heeled shoes called 'sabots' by the French. In these protections, a lady may indulge her passion for flowers at all seasons, without risk of rheumatism or chills, providing it does not actually rain or snow; and the cheering influence of the fresh air, combined with a favourite amusement, must ever operate beneficially on the mind and body in every season of the year.

Louisa Johnson, Every Lady her own Flower Gardener, 1840

Pockets are always useful in gardening – though modern ones are a pale shadow of their former magnificence:

GARDENS AND GARDENERS

In appearance great-aunt Lancilla was a very impressive old lady... Under her skirt and fastened like an apron she wore a Pocket. Only a capital letter can give an idea of the size and importance of this curious garment, which consisted of a whole array of flat, envelope-like receptacles, into which she slipped anything and everything she needed. A trowel and a small hand-fork, for instance, disappeared easily into those capacious depths, to say nothing of such trifles as stale bread for the ducks, corn for the pigeons, etc. Most people would find it difficult to walk gracefully with trowels and such knocking their ankles, but these impedimenta never seemed to interfere with her quick, yet dignified movements.

Eleanour Sinclair Rohde, *The Scented Garden*, 1931

Risley, Derbyshire

At Warley Place in Essex in the early 1900s, the idiosyncratic Ellen Willmott was creating the most famous of her three gardens where she eventually employed 104 gardeners. Their uniform consisted of

boaters (which presumably were taken off while working), in green and natural straw with a green band round them, knitted green silk ties, and navy blue aprons (which they had to remove, fold up and tuck under their arms when they went home or even when they crossed the road to get to the other part of the garden). The uniform looked very smart and may have made young gardeners feel they were entering a very grand establishment, but it could hardly have been fun to wear.

>   Audrey le Lièvre, *Miss Willmott of Warley Place*,
>   1980

Our England is a garden that is full of stately
   views,
Of borders, beds and shrubberies and lawns and
   avenues,
With statues on the terraces and peacocks strutting
   by;
But the Glory of the Garden lies in more than
   meets the eye.

For where the old thick laurels grow, along the
   thin red wall,
You find the tool- and potting-sheds which are the
   heart of all;
The cold-frames and the hot-houses, the dung-pits
   and the tanks,
The rollers, carts and drain-pipes, with the barrows
   and the planks.

And there you'll see the gardeners, the men and
   'prentice boys
Told off to do as they are bid and do it without
   noise;
For, except when seeds are planted and we shout
   to scare the birds,
The Glory of the Garden it abideth not in words.

And some can pot begonias and some can bud a
   rose,
And some are hardly fit to trust with anything that
   grows;
But they can roll and trim the lawns and sift the
   sand and loam,
For the Glory of the Garden occupieth all who come.

GARDENS AND GARDENERS

> Our England is a garden, and such gardens are
>   not made
> By singing:– 'Oh, how beautiful!' and sitting
>   in the shade,
> While better men than we go out and start their
>   working lives
> At grubbing weeds from gravel-paths with broken
>   dinner-knives...
>
> Rudyard Kipling, from 'The Glory of the Garden',
Sixty Poems, 1939

Sitting in the shade would certainly have been frowned upon by the Duke of Devonshire's head gardener Joseph Paxton, a man of exceptional energy:

I left London by the Comet Coach for Chesterfield; arrived at Chatsworth at 4.30 a.m. in the morning of the ninth of May, 1826. As no person was to be seen at that early hour, I got over the greenhouse gate by the old covered way, explored the pleasure grounds and looked round the outside of the house. I then went down to the kitchen gardens, scaled the outside wall and saw the whole of the place, set the men to work at six o'clock; then returned to Chatsworth and got Thomas Weldon to play me the water works and afterwards went to breakfast with poor dear Mrs. Gregory and her niece. The latter fell in love with me and I with her, and thus completed my first morning's work at Chatsworth before nine o'clock.

Joseph Paxton, quoted in Violet Markham, *Paxton and the Bachelor Duke*, 1935

He married his Sarah not long afterwards, and with his employer he enjoyed a lifelong relationship of mutual respect and friendship – something sadly lacking at the fictional Blandings Castle.

'Angus McAllister' said Lord Emsworth, 'is a professional gardener. I need say no more. You know as well as I do, my dear fellow, what professional gardeners are like when it is a question of moss... Moss, for some obscure reason, appears to infuriate them. It rouses their basest passions. Nature intended a yew alley to be carpeted with a mossy growth. The mossy path in the yew alley at Blandings is in true relation for colour to the trees and grassy edges; yet will you credit it that that soulless disgrace to Scotland actually wished to grub it all up and have a rolled gravel path staring up from beneath those immemorial trees! I have already told you how I was compelled to give in to him in the matter of the hollyhocks – head gardeners of any ability at all are rare in these days and one has to make concessions – but this was too much. I was perfectly friendly and civil about it. "Certainly, McAllister," I said, "you may have your gravel path if you wish. I make but one proviso, that you construct it over my dead body. Only when I am weltering in my blood on the threshold of that yew alley shall you disturb one inch of my beautiful moss. Try to remember, McAllister," I said, still quite cordially, "that you are not laying out a recreation ground in a Glasgow suburb – you are proposing to make an eyesore of what is possibly the most beautiful nook in one of the finest and oldest gardens in the United Kingdom." He made some repulsive Scotch noise at the back of his throat, and there the matter rests...'

P. G. Wodehouse, *Leave it to Psmith*, 1923

Such professional gardeners can be put out when they are beaten at their own game by the unorthodox methods of amateurs like the fictional station-master of Matching's Easy.

He was a small, elderly man with a determined-looking face and a sea voice, and it was clear he overestimated the distance of his hearers.

'Mr Darling what's head gardener up at Claverings, 'e can't get sweet peas like that, try 'ow 'e will. Tried everything 'e 'as. Sand ballast, 'e's tried. Seeds same as me. 'E came along 'ere only the other day, 'e did, and 'e says to me, 'e says, "darned 'f I can see why a station-master should beat a professional gardener at 'is own game," 'e says, "but you do. And in your orf time, too, so's to speak," 'e says. "I've tried sile," 'e says –' . . .

'I says to 'im, "there's one thing you 'aven't tried," I says,' the station-master continued, raising his voice by a Herculean feat still higher . . . 'I says to 'im, I says, "'ave you tried the vibritation of the trains?" I says. "That's what you 'aven't tried, Mr Darling. That's what you *can't* try," I says. "But you rest assured that that's the secret of my sweet peas," I says, "nothing less and nothing more than the vibritation of the trains."'

H. G. Wells, *Mr Britling Sees It Through*, 1916

All gardeners have their own eccentricities but thankfully few behave like Mr W. E. Gumbleton, a talented Victorian horticulturist of Belgrove, County Cork. His visit to the Royal Botanic Garden, Glasnevin, is recalled by its Keeper.

In the Aquatic House, Mr Gumbleton took me to task severely for my pronunciation of the name of a plant, emphasizing his remarks by banging his umbrella on the flags. Mr Woodall wanted to see the Orchids; Mr Gumbleton wanted to see the florists' flowers out-of-doors; Mr Bennett-Poë was willing to go anywhere and kept the peace between the other two. In front of the range, Mr Gumbleton denounced a plant – I cannot now recall its name – as 'a Tush plant', his term for any plant he did not like, and proceeded to beat it to bits with his umbrella, a habit of which he gave evidence in other gardens, where the owners had sufficient courage to rate him soundly. I was too timid to do more than mildly remonstrate and bemoan the loss of a recently arrived plant. In 1907, in company with the late Mr William Watson, of Kew, I visited Mr Gumbleton at Belgrove, and there Mr Watson was able to witness a similar atrocity performed by Mr Gumbleton with, I believe, the same umbrella, on one of his own plants amidst ejaculations of 'Tush! Tush!'

> Sir Frederick Moore, letter in *The Gardener's Chronicle*, 13 March 1937

Sir Frank Crisp, the wealthy Victorian solicitor who owned Friar Park in Henley, was a garden joker.

He worked hard, and earned and ate much, and diverted his mind from company promoting by erecting sham Swiss mountains and passes, decorated by china chamois, which had to be spied through Zeiss glasses, and elaborate caves and underground lakes, lit up with electricity, and festooned with artificial grapes, spiders and other monsters. He took his visitors round the caves and the garden (which was also filled with china hobgoblins and other surprises), dressed in a long frockcoat and top hat and with a large umbrella in his hands, as if he was walking to his Throgmorton Street office, his manner perfectly serious when warning one against the danger of a monstrous spider alighting on one's hat. We were then floating in small boats on the underground lake, lit up by electric light.

> Lady Ottoline Morrell, in *Ottoline, The Early Memoirs of Lady Ottoline Morrell*, ed. Robert Gathorne-Hardy, 1963

Dean Hole, famous nineteenth-century rosarian, owned to a 'wild passionate affection' for animal manure.

Returning on a summer's afternoon from a parochial walk, I inferred from wheel-tracks on my carriage-drive that callers had been and gone. I expected to find cards in the hall, and I saw that the horses had kindly left theirs on the gravel. At that moment one of those

> 'Grim spirits in the air,
> Who grin to see us mortals grieve,
> And dance at our despair,'

fiendishly suggested to my mind an economical desire to utilise the souvenir before me. I looked around and listened; no sight, no sound, of humanity. I fetched the largest fire-shovel I could find, and was carrying it bountifully laden through an archway cut in a high hedge of yews, and towards a favourite tree of 'Charles Lefebvre,' when I suddenly confronted three ladies, 'who had sent round the carriage, hearing that I should soon be at home, and were admiring my beautiful roses'. It may be said with the strictest regard to veracity, that they saw nothing that day which they admired, in the primary meaning of the word, so much as myself and fire-shovel; and I am equally sure that no rose in my garden had a redder complexion than my own.

Dean Hole, *A Book About Roses*, 1870

The composer Constant Lambert visiting Reinshaw, the Sitwells' Derbyshire home, was breakfasting alone in the dining-room when he caught this unusual first glimpse of his host, old Sir George.

... looking towards the window opposite him, he was amazed to see the distinguished, bearded, medieval face of an elderly gentleman, crowned with a large grey felt hat, pass just outside, in a horizontal position – as if he had fallen prone and was about to raise himself – and holding a malacca walking-stick in the mouth. The vision of this venerable figure proceeding on all fours was startling in its unexpectedness, and strongly recalled to the mind of him who beheld it Blake's picture of Nebuchadnezzar, though it is true that the Babylonish king was notably less spruce in appearance, and that his counterpart was plainly English and lacked those memorable nails shaped like the claws of birds. Constant hurried to the window, looked out – and realised what was happening. It was – it must be – my father, at work, and carrying his cane in this unusual manner in order to observe the views and measure from the new level – for he intended to drop the lawn three or four feet, and so, in his present position, was at the height of a man standing at the altitude he planned ...

Osbert Sitwell, *Laughter in the Next Room*, 1949

Gardeners also have their pet hates:

I have a horror of those leaden cupids who illustrate, so gruesomely, the ultimate horrors of Bright's disease in many surburban pleasaunces. I cannot bear those grim terra cotta pelicans that peer sharply from thickets of bamboos in the grounds of tasteless Midland persons.

Beverley Nichols, *Down the Garden Path*, 1932

I, for my part, do not like images cut out in juniper or other garden stuff; they be for children.

Francis Bacon, *Of Gardens*, 1625

I can admire and enjoy most flowers, but just a few I positively dislike. Collarette dahlias and those superlatively double African marigolds that look like indiarubber bath sponges offend me most of all. I dislike the cheap thin texture of godetias almost as much as I do the sinful magenta streaks and splotches that run in the blood of that family. I loathe celosias equally with dyed pampas-grass; and coxcombs, and spotty, marbled, double balsams I should like to smash up with a coalhammer; and certain great flaunting mauve and purple cattleyas cloy my nose and annoy my eye till I conjure up a vision of them expiating their gaudy double-dyed wickedness with heads impaled on stiff wires like those of criminals on pikes, in a sea of *Asparagus sprengeri*, and forming the bouquet presented to the wife of a provincial Mayor on the occasion of his opening the new sewage works.

E. A. Bowles, *My Garden in Summer*, 1914

The annual sunflower:

Fit for nothing but very extensive shrubberies, where, seen from a distance, the sight may endure it.

William Cobbett, *The English Gardener*, 1829

... the chrysanthemum more almost than any other flower suffers from that megalomania which is the British gardener's sole ideal of beauty. All he cares for is to get a thing large; farewell colour, fragrance, elegance, so long as you have a vast draggled head that looks like a moulting mop dipped in stale lobster-sauce. The result is a show chrysanthemum.

Reginald Farrer, *My Rock Garden*, 1907

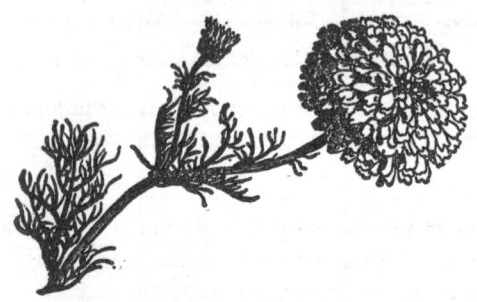

Enthusiasms are diverse too. Some, like old Matthew Shore, fill their gardens entirely with flowers...

He is what is becoming scarcer every day, a florist of the first order, and of the old school... of thirty or forty years back, the reign of pinks, tulips, auriculas, and ranunculuses, when the time and skill of the gardener were devoted to produce, in the highest imaginable perfection, a variety of two or three favoured tribes. The whole of this large garden, for the potatoes and cabbages have been forced to retreat to a nook in the orchard, dug up in their behoof – the whole ample garden is laid out in long beds, like those in a nursery ground, filled with these precious flowers, of the rarest sorts and in the highest culture; and as I have arrived in the midst of the hyacinth, auricula, and anemone season, with the tulips just opening, I may consider myself in great luck to see what is called, in gardening language, 'so grand a show'. It is worth something, too, to see Matthew's delight, half compounded of vanity and kindness, as he shows them, mixed with courteous offers of seedlings and offsets, and biographical notices of the more curious flowers...

Mary Russell Mitford, *Our Village*, 1824–32

... while others are like Robert, an old Scots gardener who

scorned all flowers together. They were but garnishings, childish toys, trifling ornaments for ladies' chimney-shelves. It was towards his cauliflowers and peas and cabbage that his heart grew warm. His preference for the more useful growths was such that cabbages were found invading the flower-plots, and an outpost of savoys was once discovered in the centre of the lawn.

Robert Louis Stevenson, *Memories and Portraits*, 1890

His opinions are shared by a present-day gardener.

Vegetables and fruit are my province. I will spend any amount of time and energy on the growing of those. There is a streak of the puritan in me, which chides me that time spent on things which merely flower and possibly smell nice, are merely ornamental, is time frittered away.

Susan Hill, *The Magic Apple Tree*, 1982

The garden can be a status symbol or a way of life:

If the regular City man, who leaves Lloyd's at five o'clock, and drives home to Hackney, Clapton, Stamford-hill, or elsewhere, can be said to have any daily recreation beyond his dinner, it is in his garden. He never does anything to it with his own hands; but he takes great pride in it notwithstanding; and if you are desirous of paying your addresses to the youngest daughter, be sure to be in raptures with every flower and shrub it contains ... He always takes a walk round it, before he starts for town in the morning, and is particularly anxious that the fish-pond should be kept specially neat. If you call on him on Sunday in summertime, about an hour before dinner, you will find him sitting in an armchair, on the lawn behind the house, with a straw hat on, reading a Sunday paper ... Beyond these occasions, his delight in his garden appears to arise more from the consciousness of possession than actual enjoyment of it...

There is another and a very different class of men, whose recreation is their garden. An individual of this class, resides some short distance from town – say in the Hampstead-road, or the Kilburn-road, or any other road where the houses are small and neat, and have little slips of back garden. He and his wife... have occupied the same house ever since he retired from business twenty years ago...

In fine weather the old gentleman is almost constantly in the garden; and when it is too wet to go into it, he will look out of the window at it, by the hour together. He has always something to do there, and you will see him digging, and sweeping, and cutting, and planting, with manifest delight. In spring-time, there is no end to the sowing of seeds, and sticking little bits of wood over them, with labels, which look like epitaphs to their memory; and in the evening, when the sun has gone down, the perseverance with which he lugs a great watering-pot about is perfectly astonishing... The old lady is very fond of flowers, as the hyacinth-glasses in the parlour-window, and geranium-pots in the little front court, testify. She takes great pride in the garden too: and when one of the four fruit-trees produces rather a larger gooseberry than usual, it is carefully preserved under a wine-glass on the sideboard, for the edification of visitors, who are duly informed that Mr. So-and-so planted the tree which produced it, with his own hands.

Charles Dickens, *Sketches by Boz*, 1836

Equally green-fingered was twelve-year-old Dickon, exploring here with young Mary the secret garden she has found at Misselthwaite Manor.

He stepped over to the nearest tree – an old, old one with grey lichen all over its bark, but upholding a curtain of tangled sprays and branches. He took a thick knife out of his pocket and opened one of its blades.

'There's lots o' dead wood as ought to be cut out,' he said. 'An' there's a lot o' old wood, but it made some new last year. This here's a new bit,' and he touched a shoot which looked brownish-green instead of hard, dry grey.

Mary touched it herself in an eager, reverent way.

'That one?' she said. 'Is that one quite alive – quite?'

Dickon curved his wide, smiling mouth.

'It's as wick as you or me,' he said; and Mary remembered that Martha had told her that 'wick' meant 'alive' or 'lively'...

They went from bush to bush and from tree to tree. He was very strong and clever with his knife and knew how to cut the dry and dead wood away, and could tell when an unpromising bough or twig had still green life in it. In the course of half an hour, Mary thought she could tell too, and when he cut through a lifeless-looking branch she would cry out joyfully under her breath when she caught sight of the least shade of moist green. The spade, and hoe, and fork were very useful. He showed her how to use the fork while he dug about the roots with the spade and stirred the earth and let the air in.

Frances Hodgson Burnett, *The Secret Garden*, 1911

Those with little aptitude or inclination for gardening have to rely on such help as they can find:

Such a gardener as will conscionably, quietly, and patiently travel in your orchard, God shall crown the labours of his hands with joyfulness, and make the clouds drop fatness upon your trees; he will provoke your love, and earn his wages and fees belonging to his place. The house being served, fallen fruit, superfluity of herbs, and flowers, seed, grass, sets, and besides all other of that fruit which your bountiful hand shall reward him withall, will much augment his wages...

William Lawson, *A New Orchard and Garden*, 1618

The modern jobbing gardener does not always wait to be offered his perks. Miles Kington's 'Let's Parler Franglais' column in Punch *reveals his worst excesses.*

Avec le Part-Time Gardener

MONSIEUR: Bonjour, Twining.

JARDINIER: Arrh.

MONSIEUR: Everything est lovely dans le jardin, then?

JARDINIER: Arrh.

MONSIEUR: Bon bon. Bon... Pourquoi la magnolia a disparu?

JARDINIER: Pas disparu, monsieur. Je l'ai prunée un peu.

MONSIEUR: Vous l'avez beaucoup prunée. Drastiquement. C'est maintenant un stump.

JARDINIER: Elle aime le hard pruning. Elle adore ça.

MONSIEUR: Hmm... Où sont mes dahlias?

JARDINIER: Ils sont finished.

MONSIEUR: La semaine passée, elles n'étaient pas started.

JARDINIER: C'est une saison désastreuse pour les dahlias.

MONSIEUR: Hmm... Je ne vois pas le flowering cherry.

JARDINIER: Ce n'est pas flowering maintenant.

MONSIEUR: Je ne vois pas un non-flowering cherry.

JARDINIER: Ah. Well. Non. Le cherry n'aimait pas sa position. Il détestait le soil. Donc, je l'ai transplanté.

MONSIEUR: Transplanté? Où ça?

JARDINIER: Dans mon jardin.

MONSIEUR: Dans votre...?

JARDINIER: C'est dans vos meilleurs interêts.

MONSIEUR: Oh, well... Où est le lawn?

JARDINIER: Lawn, squire? Oh, le patch d'herbe. Je l'ai excavé pour y planter les oignons et les spuds, comme vous avez dit.

MONSIEUR: Moi? J'ai dit ça?

JARDINIER: Absolument. Pas une ombre de doute. 'Ce damned lawn,' vous avez dit.

MONSIEUR: Et les chaises longues qui étaient sur le lawn? Et le croquet? Et le mower et la summer maison?

JARDINIER: Tous en shocking condition. J'en ai disposé.

MONSIEUR: Correctez-moi si ja'i tort, mais dans la semaine vous avez rémové les fleurs et les arbres, ruiné le lawn et auctionné ma furniture. Right?

JARDINIER: Je fais mon job. C'est tout.

MONSIEUR: Ha!

JARDINIER: Il est très difficile de trouver les jobbing gardeners, vous savez. *Très* difficile. Espéciellement pour peanuts. Si vous n'aimez pas mon travail...

MONSIEUR: OK, OK. Sorry si j'ai été hasty.

JARDINIER: J'accepte vos apologies.

MONSIEUR: Aujourd'hui, si vous faites seulement le tidying-up...

JARDINIER: Just laissez-moi à mes devices, OK, squire? C'est très difficile avec le criticisme constant.

MONSIEUR: Right. D'accord. Sorry. Maintenant il me faut aller au travail.

JARDINIER: Et moi aussi.

Punch, 19 August 1981

Some lean on their spades overmuch:

Those who have employed a jobbing gardener will realize at once that 'contemplative', when applied to a gardener, is not a purely commendatory epithet...

Jason Hill, *The Contemplative Gardener*, 1940

while others

turn up on the appointed day of the week whatever the conditions of rain, frost, snow or tempest. Only in April and May are they confined to their beds... Pruning, spraying, pricking out and every unpleasant job they avoid by saying 'I baint no gardener'. They will get rid of precious, purchased dung at a colossal depth on a tiny area. In all matters connected with planting and weather they are firm believers in the moon, and the moon is never in an auspicious phase.

Ralph Wightman, in *A Book of Gardens*, 1963

GARDENS AND GARDENERS

Middle class households sometimes imposed extra demands on the long-suffering gardener:

> Jonathan Jo
> Has a mouth like an 'O'
> And a wheelbarrow full of surprises;
> If you ask for a bat,
> Or for something like that,
> He has got it, whatever the size is.
>
> If you're wanting a ball,
> It's no trouble at all;
> Why, the more that you ask for, the merrier –
> Like a hoop and a top,
> And a watch that won't stop,
> And some sweets, and an Aberdeen terrier.
>
> Jonathan Jo
> Has a mouth like an 'O',
> But this is what makes him so funny:
> If you give him a smile,
> Only once in a while,
> *Then he never expects any money!*
>
> A. A. Milne, *Christopher Robin Verses*, 1932

Gardens

THE GARDEN

> It is a gesture against the wild,
> The ungovernable sea of grass;
> A place to remember love in,
> To be lonely for a while;
> To forget the voices of children
> Calling from a locked room;
> To substitute for the care
> Of one querulous human
> Hundreds of dumb needs.
>
> It is the old kingdom of man:
> Answering to their names
> Out of the soil the buds come,
> The silent detonations
> Of power wielded without sin.
>
> R. S. Thomas, in A Book of Gardens, 1963

I never had any other desire so strong, and so like to covetousness, as that one which I have had always, that I might be master at last of a small house and large garden, with very moderate conveniences joined to them, and there dedicate the remainder of my life to the culture of them, and study of nature ... yet I stick still in the inn of an hired house and garden, among weeds and rubbish; and without that pleasantest work of human industry, the improvement of something which we call (not very properly, but yet we call) our own.

Abraham Cowley, in John Evelyn's Kalendarium Hortense, 1666 (1706 ed.)

While home ownership is certainly a spur to self-improvement, the born gardener will attempt to im-

prove his surroundings wherever he is, whether in a tied cottage or a prison.

> To every cot the lord's indulgent mind
> Has a small space for garden ground assign'd;
> Here – till return of morn dismiss'd the farm –
> The careful peasant plies the sinewy arm,
> Warm'd as he works, and casts his look around
> On every foot of that improving ground;
> It is his own he sees; his master's eye
> Peers not about, some secret fault to spy;
> Nor voice severe is there, nor censure known; –
> Hope, profit, pleasure – they are all his own.
> Here grow the humble chives, and, hard by them,
> The leek with crown globose and reedy stem;
> High climb his pulse in many an even row;
> Deep strike the ponderous roots in soil below;
> And herbs of potent smell and pungent taste
> Give a warm relish to the night's repast;
> Apples and cherries grafted by his hand,
> And cluster'd nuts for neighbouring market stand.
>
> Nor thus concludes his labour; near the cot,
> The reed-fence rises round some fav'rite spot;
> Where rich carnations, pinks with purple eyes,
> Proud hyacinths, the least some florist's prize,
> Tulips tall-stemm'd, and pounced auriculas rise.
>
> George Crabbe, from *The Parish Register*, 1863

The poet and essayist Leigh Hunt, imprisoned for seditious libel in Surrey Gaol, contrived to have a garden in

a little yard outside the room, railed off from another belonging to the neighbouring ward. This yard I shut in with green palings, adorned it with a trellis, bordered it with a thick bed of earth from a nursery, and even contrived to have a grass plot. The earth I filled with flowers and young trees. There was an apple-tree from which we managed to get a pudding the second year. As to my flowers, they were allowed to be perfect.

Thomas Moore, who came to see me with Lord Byron, told me he had seen no such heart's-ease ... Here I wrote and read in fine weather, sometimes under an awning. In autumn, my trellises were hung with scarlet-runners, which added to the flowery investment.

Leigh Hunt, *Autobiography*, 1850

A garden can be as revealing a clue to personality as the inside of a house or handbag:

The garden had to be put in order, and each sister had a quarter of the little plot to do what she liked with. Hannah used to say, 'I'd know which each of them gardings belonged to, ef I see 'em in Chiny'; and so she might, for the girls' tastes differed as much as their characters. Meg's had roses and heliotrope, myrtle, and a little orange-tree in it. Jo's bed was never alike two seasons, for she was always trying experiments; this year it was to be a plantation of sunflowers, the seeds of which cheerful and aspiring plant were to feed 'Aunt Cockle-top' and her family of chicks. Beth had old-fashioned, fragrant flowers in her garden, sweet peas and mignonette, larkspur, pinks, pansies, and southernwood, with chickweed for the bird and catnip for the pussies. Amy had a bower in hers – rather small and earwiggy, but very pretty to look at – with honeysuckles and morning-glories hanging their coloured horns and bells in graceful wreaths all over it; tall white lilies, delicate ferns, and as many brilliant, picturesque plants as would consent to blossom there.

Louisa May Alcott, *Little Women*, 1868

Problems can arise, however, when two people attempt to express their differing preferences in one garden. Here a fictional garden owned by Colonel Rendezvous, a military man with a passion for physical fitness and discipline, is described by an aquaintance:

'They have the tidiest garden in Essex,' said Manning. 'It's not Mrs Rendezvous' fault that it is so. Mrs Rendezvous, as a matter of fact, has a taste for the picturesque. She just puts the things about in groups in the beds. She wants them, she says, to grow anyhow. She desires a romantic disorder. But she never gets it. When he walks down the path all the plants dress instinctively... And there's a tree near their gate; it used to be a willow. You can ask any old man in the village. But ever since Rendezvous took the place it's been trying to present arms. With the most extraordinary results. I was passing the other day with old Windershin. "You see that there old poplar," he said. "It's a willow," said I. "No," he said, "it did used to be a willow before Colonel Rendezvous he came. But now it's a poplar."... And, by Jove, it *is* a poplar!'

H. G. Wells, *Mr Britling Sees It Through*, 1916

The sole owner of a garden is free to indulge his idiosyncracies:

Mole reached down a lantern from a nail on the wall and lit it, and the Rat, looking round him, saw that they were in a sort of forecourt. A garden-seat stood on one side of the door, and on the other, a roller; for the Mole, who was a tidy animal when at home, could not stand having his ground kicked up by other animals into little runs that ended in earth-heaps. On the walls hung wire baskets with ferns in them, alternating with brackets carrying plaster statuary – Garibaldi, and the infant Samuel, and Queen Victoria, and other heroes of modern Italy. Down one side of the forecourt ran a skittle-alley, with benches along it and little wooden tables marked with rings that hinted at beer-mugs. In the middle was a small round pond containing goldfish and surrounded by a cockle-shell border. Out of the centre of the pond rose a fanciful erection clothed in more cockle-shells and topped by a large silvered glass ball that reflected everything all wrong and had a very pleasing effect.

Kenneth Grahame, *The Wind in the Willows*, 1908

Statuary and waterworks were on a larger scale at Bretby, Lord Chesterfield's Derbyshire estate:

But that which is most admired – and justly so to be – by all persons and excite their curiosity to come and see is the gardens and waterworks; out of the billiard room the first was with gravel walks and a large fountain in the middle with flower pots and greens set round the brim of the fountains that are paved with stone; you see but one garden at a time; the pipes in the fountains play very finely, some of a great height, some flushes the water about, then you come to a descent of several steps which discovers another fine garden with fountains playing through pipes, beset on the banks with all sort of greens and flower trees dwarfs honeysuckles in a round tuft growing upright and all sorts of flower trees and greens finely cut and exactly kept; in one garden there are three fountains wherein stands great statues, each side on their pedestals is a dial, one for the sun, the other a clock which by the water work is moved and strikes the hours and chimes the quarters, and when they please play Lilibolaro on the chimes – all this I heard when I was there – on one side of this garden is a half compass with a breast wall on which are high iron pallisadoes divided with several pillars, stone with images on their tops; about two yards distance this opens to view the park and a sort of canal or pond which is in it of a good bigness; beyond this garden is a row of orange and lemon trees set in the ground, of a man's height and pretty big, full of flowers and some large fruit almost ripe...

The Journeys of Celia Fiennes, 1698

In contrast, an example of what we might now call wilderness gardening:

I have several acres about my house, which I call my garden, and which a skilful gardener would not know what to call. It is a confusion of kitchen and parterre, orchard and flower garden, which lie so mixed and interwoven with one another, that if a foreigner who had seen nothing of our country should be conveyed into my garden at his first landing, he would look upon it as a natural wilderness, and one of the uncultivated parts of our country. My flowers grow up in several parts of the garden in the greatest luxuriancy and profusion. I am so far from being fond of any particular one, by reason of its rarity, that if I meet with any one in a field which pleases me, I give it a place in my garden. By this means, when a stranger walks with me, he is surprised to see several large spots of ground covered with ten thousand different colours, and has often singled out flowers that he might have met with under a common hedge, in a field, or in a meadow, as some of the greatest beauties of the place... There is the same irregularity in my plantations, which run into as great a wildness as their natures will permit... I must not omit, that there is a fountain rising in the upper part of my garden, which forms a little wandering rill, and administers to the pleasure as well as the plenty of the place. I have so conducted it, that it visits most of my plantations, and have taken particular care to let it run in the same manner as it would do in an open field, so that it generally passes through banks of violets and primroses, plats of willow, or other plants, that seem to be of its own producing.

Joseph Addison, *The Spectator*, 6 September 1712

GARDENS

An English family's garden in Bengal, India, has a river as the background to its exotic plants and wildlife:

It was a beautiful garden. The poinsettias grew round the plinth of the house, huge scarlet-fingered flowers with milk sap in their stems... Below the poinsettias was the plumbago; it made hedges of nursery pale blue and the flowerbeds it bordered would later be full of the pansies and verbena and mignonette that were now in seed pans in a seed-table made of bamboo. Along the paths were ranged pots of violets that held the dew. Other pots of chrysanthemums were on the verandah and in a double phalanx down the steps. These chrysanthemums had mammoth heads of flowers that were white and yellow and bronze and pink; some of them were larger than the children's heads. Later, in their place, there would be potted petunias.

The lawns rolled away to the river under the trees, but there were flowers, bougainvillaeas, that spread themselves into clumps and up the trees, orange, purple, magenta and cerise, like Bea's hair ribbon; there were Maréchal-Niel turrets with their small lemon-yellow roses, and other roses in the rose-garden, and bushes of the small white Bengali roses tinged with pink. There were standard hibiscus that were out already in pinks, and creams and yellows and reds, and morning glory and other creepers, on the house, over the porch, along screens, up trees; jasmine and orange-keyed begonias, passion flowers and quis-qualis that would flower in January and the spring; now there was only the pink-and-white sandwich creeper out and Bea's bridal creeper over the gate. There were squirrels and lizards in the garden and birds: bulbuls and kingfishers and doves and the magpie robin and sunbirds and tree pies and wagtails and hawks. Birds are little live landmarks and more truthful than flowers; they cannot be transplanted, nor grafted, nor turned blue and pink. The birds were in the flavour of that garden, as the white paddy birds and the vultures were part of the flavour of the fields, and the circling kites and the kingfishers of the river; the garden was full of swallow-tail butterflies bigger than the sunbirds and of Bogey's insects and Bogey's ants; no one really knew the insects except Bogey. At night there were sometimes jackals on the lawn and fireflies, and there was a bush that used to fill the whole house with its scent in the darkness, a bush called Lady-of-the-Night.

Rumer Godden, *The River*, 1946

More traditional borders surrounded an English farmhouse:

The garden borders are discreetly furnished, so that they are now as clouds in the neighbourhood of the sun, doing it honour by their liveries. They are populous with sunflowers, hollyhocks (tall, solemn halberds at evening, guarding the outmost edge and held up mysteriously), red-hot pokers rising out of a lake of rose of Sharon and nasturtium, into which run promontories and peninsulas of snapdragon, rocket, Shirley poppy, carnation and phlox of every hue that white and red confederate can invent; here and there fuchsia trees in rivers of autumn crocus, great poppies and evening primrose, and at their feet, like long, coloured shadows stretching away, red flax and pansies and the recurved stonecrop which the tortoise-shell butterfly loves. These bodies of colour change year by year – in one autumn the pansies make a long, curled, purple dragon among all the rest; but always the taller flowers look as if stopped short in the mazes of a dance which is soon to be resumed. Between these two borders are two little lawns divided by a path, whereon the fanciful might see a little beam of the house's influence in the peacock butterfly that returns continually to one stone, settling there as the wanton light cast on ceiling and wall by a raised glass settles when the glass is put down.

It is not a rich or choice garden, though a fitting one. Yet an earlier head of the farmer's family ... was so

GARDENS

much enamoured of the flowers and the house that he came, towards the end of his life, to think himself over-worldly in his esteem of them, but failed to overcome it, and, a little before his death, in the free wanderings of his mind, announced that he saw Paradise, and that it was even as his garden was, 'nasturtiums and all, Jacob' (which was a thrust at the said son, a disliker of those flowers) – except that the vain-glorious new carnations were not there.

Edward Thomas, *The Heart of England*, 1906

Other gardens were similarly loved by their owners:

Inside Bag End, Bilbo and Gandalf were sitting at the open window of a small room looking out west on to the garden. The late afternoon was bright and peaceful. The flowers glowed red and golden: snapdragons and sunflowers, and nasturtians [*sic*] trailing all over the turf walls and peeping in at the round windows.

'How bright your garden looks!' said Gandalf.

'Yes,' said Bilbo. 'I am very fond indeed of it...'

J. R. R. Tolkien, *The Lord of the Rings*, 1954

The pride of my heart, and the delight of my eyes is my garden... Fancy a small plot of ground, with a pretty low irregular cottage at one end; a large granary, divided from the dwelling by a little court running along one side; and a long thatched shed, open towards the garden, and supported by wooden pillars, on the other. The bottom is bounded, half by an old wall, and half by an old paling, over which we see a pretty distance of woody hills. The house, granary, wall, and paling, are covered with vines, cherry-trees, roses, honeysuckles, and jessamines, with great clusters of tall hollyhocks running up between them; a large elder overhanging the little gate, and a magnificent bay-tree, such a tree as shall scarcely be matched in these parts, breaking with its beautiful conical form the horizontal lines of the buildings. This is my garden; and the long pillared shed, the sort of rustic arcade which runs along one side, parted from the flower-beds by a row of rich geraniums, is our out-of-door drawing-room.

Mary Russell Mitford, *Our Village*, 1824–32

Unhappily, a garden is an ephemeral creation:

Arrived at Three Mile Cross, it was no surprise to find it no longer recognisable as the hamlet described in *Our Village*... The cottage has been much altered since Miss Mitford's time, and the open space once occupied by the beloved garden is now filled with buildings, including a corrugated-iron dissenting chapel.

W. H. Hudson, *Afoot in England*, 1909

A similar fate befell a Kelso garden...

The little cottage in which I lived with poor Aunt Jenny is still standing but the great garden is divided betwixt three proprietors. Its huge Platanus tree is withered, I was told, in the same season which was fatal to so many of the species. It was cut down – The yew hedges, labyrinths, wildernesses, and other marks that it had once been the abode of one of the Millers connected with the author of the Gardener's Dictionary... are all obliterated and the place as common and vulgar as may be.

Sir Walter Scott, *Journal*, August 1827

GARDENS

... and the grander, though equally beloved garden of the poet William Shenstone:

the Leasowes ... has been sadly changed since Shenstone's time, by a succession of tasteless and ignorant proprietors; its hedges clipped, its dark serpentine walks untwisted and cleared, its cascades converted into dry ditches, its root-houses, obelisks, and seats torn down or turned into fuel, its memorial urns kicked down hill, its fawns robbed of their heads; and those ingenious inscriptions on which the poet so much prided himself ... blotted out ... *Sic transit gloria mundi* – of that little world of beauty and taste which Shenstone, with such admirable skill, collected around him.

Revd George Gilfillan, in his introduction to Poetical Works of William Shenstone, 1854

LINES FOR A COUNTRY GARDEN

The quality of light within this garden,
As from a concentration here, has grown
So rich, it is as if the air has taken
Gold from the sun or silver from the moon
And holds them finely particled in one
Suspended pouring that is never done.

So in the sunlight now this cherry-bark
Glows like old leather, and warmth equally
Lies hidden in the wallflower's velvet dark
Or blazes from the lilac's lazuli;
Even the rust upon this wrought-iron seat
Is turned to burnish by the golden heat.

And surely this shall last when they are gone
Who kept this garden. If love can endure
Shall it not do so here, something work on,
Making its own memorial of air?
Something that says: This is a place to bless,
Though all the world return to wilderness.

D. J. Sutton, in The Countryman, Summer 1967

GARDENS AND GARDENERS

Traditional cottage gardens provided vital produce for the family.

Went to the Bronith. People at work in the orchard gathering up the windfall apples for early cider. The smell of the apples very strong... Called on the old soldier. He was with his wife in the garden digging and gathering red potatoes which turned up very large and sound, no disease, and no second growth, an unusual thing this year. The great round red potatoes lay thick, fresh and clean on the dark newly turned mould. I sat down on the stones by the spring and the old soldier came and sat down on the stones by me while his wife went on picking up the red potatoes... Mary Morgan brought me some apples, Sam's Crabs and Quinin's. The spring trickled and tinkled behind us and a boy from the keeper's cottage came to draw water in a blue and white jug.

It was very quiet and peaceful in the old soldier's garden as we sat by the spring while the sun grew low and gilded the apples in the trees which he had planted, and the keeper's wife moved about in the garden below, and we heard the distant shots at partridges.

I dug up the half row of potatoes for him which he had left unfinished.

Revd Francis Kilvert, *Diary*, 21 September 1870

... an old apple tree in the garden generally made the rent the garden was large for a poor man and my father managed to dig it night and morning before the hours of labour and lost no time He then did well but the young farmer that succeeded our old landlord raised the rent and the next year made four tenements of the house leaving us a corner of one room on a floor for three guineas a year and a little slip of the garden which was divided into four parts but as my father had been an old tenant he gave him the choice of his share and he retained our old apple tree Tho the ground was good for nothing yet the tree still befriended us and made shift to make up the greater part of our rent...

John Clare, *Autobiography*, 1793–1824

Higher in the rural social scale came the Postmistress. At Candleford Green (a fictional village based on Fringford in North Oxfordshire) she ran the Smithy too and could afford help in the garden – which was also occasionally tended by Matthew the foreman-blacksmith and his three shoeing-smiths.

Narrow paths between high, built-up banks supporting flower borders, crowded with jonquils, auriculas, forget-me-nots and other spring flowers, led from one part of the garden to another. One winding path led to the earth closet in its bower of nut-trees halfway down the garden, another to the vegetable garden and on to the rough grass plot before the beehives. Between each section were thick groves of bushes with ferns and capers and Solomon's seal, so closed in that the long, rough grass there was always damp. Wasted ground, a good gardener might have said, but delightful in its cool, green shadiness.

Nearer the house was a portion given up entirely to flowers, not growing in beds or borders, but crammed together in an irregular square, where they bloomed in half-wild profusion. There were rose bushes there and lavender and rosemary and a bush apple-tree which bore little red and yellow streaked apples in later summer, and Michaelmas daisies and red-hot pokers and old-fashioned pompom dahlias in autumn and peonies and pinks already budding.

An old man in the village came one day a week to till the vegetable garden, but the flower garden was no one's especial business. Miss Lane herself would occasionally pull on a pair of wash-leather gloves and transplant a few seedlings; Matthew would pull up a weed or stake a plant as he passed, and the smiths, once a year, turned out of the shop to dig between the roots and cut down dead canes. Betweenwhiles the flowers grew just as they would in crowded masses, perfect in their imperfection.

Flora Thompson, *Lark Rise to Candleford*, 1939

In contrast to this haphazard homeliness is the grandeur of the Villa Torlonia garden at Frascati:

... a place of mysterious silence, of low-weeping fountains and muffled footfalls; a garden of sleep. The gates are on a lower level, and athwart the rose-tangled slope to the left the architect has thrown five great slanting staircases of stone, broad enough and splendid enough to carry an army of guests to the plateau above. But this is now a solitude, a mournful ilex *bosco* with cross walks and mossy fountains shaped like the baluster of some great sundial. From the central stairway, not far from the house, a broader opening in the woodland leads to a lawn and pool below the great cascade. In front is a long cliff crowned with ilex forest and faced with a frontispiece of moss-grown arches and bubbling fountains. The main fall drops from a balcony between two tall umbrageous ilexes which rise on either hand like the horns of an Addisonian periwig; from basin to basin it drops in a silver fringe, held in by low serpentine walls that curve and re-curve like the arches of a bridge or the edges of a shell. Through vaults on either hand, long winding stairways follow the curves, the masonry is choked with ferns, the steps with weeds, and riotous water-plants crowd upon the ledges or thrust green juicy stems through the scum which has gathered in the corners of the pools. At the top, in a small irregular clearing walled by wild ilex wood and wilder tangle of flowering shrubs, is a balustraded basin in the form of a great *quatrefoil*. Gold-red fish gleam in the sea-green water, which reflects soft foliage and lichened stone and patches of pearly light; in the centre a huge cylinder of moss supports the silvery feathers of a fountain; it is an enchanted pool in a fairy woodland. But the traveller who has wandered here alone on a drowsy afternoon does not listen to the trickle of the fountain and the murmuring of the bees. From below the threshold of the mind a strange sense of hidden danger oppresses him, an instinct neither to be reasoned with nor to be understood. Can there be brigands yet in the forest heights, or is the place haunted by the shades of the soldiers who once fell in battle about the pool? He waits and wrestles with his folly, then sadly descending the slippery stairways leaves cooling fount and shaded alley for the torrid sunshine of the outer world.

It is death to sleep in the garden.

Sir George Sitwell, *On the Making of Gardens*, 1909

The Palladian Bridge, Wilton, Wiltshire

Death in various forms haunts the mad Dr Shatterhand's garden, as James Bond learns in a briefing for a dangerous job there:

'... his poison garden has become the most desirable site for suicides in the whole of Japan ... a last delicious, ruminative walk, perhaps hand-in-hand with your lover, through the beautiful groves. And finally the great gamble, the game of *pachinko* the Japanese love so much. Which ball will have your number on it? Will your death be easy or painful? Will a Russell's Viper strike at your legs as you walk the silent, well-raked paths? Will some kindly, deadly dew fall upon you during the night as you rest under this or that gorgeous tree? Or will hunger or curiosity lead you to munch a handful of those red berries or pick one of those orange fruits? ... The place is nothing more than a *departmento* of death, its shelves laden with delicious packages of self-destruction, all given away for nothing ... Genuine visitors, botanists and so on, have to show a pass. But the suicides fight their way to the shrine across the fields and marshes, scrabble at the great walls, break their nails to gain entrance.'

Ian Fleming, *You Only Live Twice*, 1964

The peace of a real Japanese garden is described by a nineteenth-century European-born journalist, whose love of the Orient led him to settle in Japan, marry there and take up Japanese citizenship.

I do not know what human sentiment the principal division of my garden was intended to reflect; and there is none to tell me. Those by whom it was made passed away long generations ago, in the eternal transmigration of souls. But as a poem of nature it requires no interpreter ... There are large rocks in it, heavily mossed; and divers fantastic basins of stone for holding water; and stone lamps green with years; and a shachihoko, such as one sees at the peaked angles of castle roofs – a great stone fish, an idealized porpoise, with its nose in the ground and its tail in the air. There are miniature hills, with old trees upon them; and there are long slopes of green, shadowed by flowering shrubs, like river banks; and there are green knolls like islets. All these verdant elevations rise from spaces of pale yellow sand, smooth as the surface of silk and miming the curves and meanderings of a river course. These sanded spaces are not to be trodden upon; they are much too beautiful for that. The least speck of dirt would mar their effect; and it requires the trained skill of an experienced native gardener – a delightful old man he is – to keep them in perfect form. But they are traversed in various directions by lines of flat unhewn rock slabs, placed at slightly irregular distances from one another, exactly like stepping-stones across a brook. The whole effect is that of the shores of a still stream in some lovely, lonesome, drowsy place.

Lafcadio Hearn, *Glimpses of Unfamiliar Japan*, 1894

Here is rockwork of a different kind:

The ideal rock-garden must have a plan. But there are three prevailing plans, none of which are good. The first is what I may call the Almond-pudding scheme, and obtains generally, especially in the north of England. You take a round bed; you pile it up with soil; you then choose out the spikiest pinnacles of limestone you can find, and you insert them thickly with their points in the air, until the general effect is that of a tipsy-cake stuck with almonds. In this vast petrified porcupine nothing will grow except Welsh poppy, ferns and some of the uglier sedums. The second style is that of the Dog's Grave. It marks a higher stage of horticulture, and is affected by many good growers of alpines. The pudding-shape is more or less the same in both, but the stones are laid flat in the Dog's-Grave ideal. Plants will grow on this, but its scheme is so stodgy and so abhorrent to Nature that it should be discarded. The third style is that of the Devil's Lapful, and prevailed very largely when alpines first began to be used out of doors. The finest specimens of this style are to be seen in such gardens as Glasnevin and Edinburgh. The plan is simplicity itself. You take a hundred or a thousand cartloads of bald square-faced boulders. You next drop them all about absolutely anyhow; and you then plant things amongst them. The chaotic hideousness of the result is something to be remembered with shudders ever after.

Reginald Farrer, *My Rock Garden*, 1907

Rocks in their natural state make the background to an unlikely allotment site:

From the vale where the Branscombe pours its clear waters through rough masses of shingle into the sea the ground to the east rises steeply to a height of nearly five hundred feet; the cliff is thus not nearly so high as many another, but it has features of peculiar interest. Here, in some former time, there has been a landslip, a large portion of the cliff at its highest part falling below and forming a sloping mass of chalky soil mingled with huge fragments of rock, which lies like a buttress against the vertical precipice and seems to lend it support ... On this rough slope, under the shelter of the cliff, with the sea at its feet, the villagers have formed their cultivated patches. The patches, wildly irregular in form, some on such steeply sloping ground as to suggest the idea that they must have been cultivated on all fours, are divided from each other by ridges and by masses of rock, deep fissures in the earth, strips of bramble and thorn and furze bushes. Altogether the effect was very singular; the huge rough mass of jumbled rock and soil, the ruin wrought by Nature in one of her Cromwellian moods, and, scattered irregularly about its surface, the plots or patches of cultivated smoothness – potato rows, green parallel lines ruled on a grey ground, and big, blue-green, equidistant cabbage-globes – each plot with its fringe of spike-like onion leaves, crinkled parsley, and other garden herbs. Here the villagers came by a narrow, steep, and difficult path they had made, to dig in their plots; while, overhead, the gulls, careless of their presence, pass and repass wholly occupied with their own affairs.

W. H. Hudson, *Afoot in England*, 1909

GARDENS

Vegetables, flowers and fruit grow in mixed profusion in the fictional Hall Farm garden where Adam Bede strolls in search of Hetty, Farmer Poyser's pretty niece:

Adam walked by the rick-yard, at present empty of ricks, to the little wooden gate leading into the garden – once the well-tended kitchen-garden of a manor-house; now, but for the handsome brick wall with stone coping that ran along one side of it, a true farmhouse garden, with hardy perennial flowers, unpruned fruit-trees, and kitchen vegetables growing together in careless, half-neglected abundance. In that leafy, flowery, bushy time, to look for anyone in this garden was like playing at 'hide-and-seek'. There were the tall hollyhocks beginning to flower, and dazzle the eye with their pink, white, and yellow; there were the syringas and Gueldres roses, all large and disorderly for want of trimming; there were leafy walls of scarlet beans and late peas; there was a row of bushy filberts in one direction, and in another a huge apple-tree making a barren circle under its low-spreading boughs. But what signified a barren patch or two? The garden was so large. There was always a superfluity of broad beans – it took nine or ten of Adam's strides to get to the end of the uncut grass walk that ran by the side of them; and as for other vegetables, there was so much more room than was necessary for them, that in the rotation of crops a large flourishing bed of groundsel was of yearly occurrence on one spot or other. The very rose-trees, at which Adam stopped to pluck one, looked as if they grew wild; they were all huddled together in bushy masses, now flaunting with wide open petals, almost all of them the streaked pink-and-white kind, which doubtless dated from the union of the houses of York and Lancaster.

George Eliot, *Adam Bede*, 1858

Even without ornamental flowers a kitchen garden can be attractive:

GARDENS AND GARDENERS

If well managed, nothing is more beautiful than the kitchen-garden: the earliest blossoms come there: we shall in vain seek for flowering shrubs in March, and early in April, to equal the peaches, nectarines, apricots, and plums; late in April, we shall find nothing to equal the pear and the cherry; and, in May, the dwarf, or espalier, apple-trees, are just so many immense garlands of carnations. The walks are unshaded: they are not greasy or covered with moss, in the spring of the year, like those in the shrubberies: to watch the progress of crops is by no means unentertaining to any rational creature; and the kitchen-garden gives you all this long before the ornamental part of the garden affords you any thing worth looking at.

William Cobbett, *The English Gardener*, 1829

I have always thought a kitchen-garden a more pleasant sight than the finest orangery, or artificial green-house. I love to see every thing in its perfection, and am more pleased to survey my rows of coleworts and cabbages, with a thousand nameless pot-herbs, springing up in their full fragrancy and verdure, than to see the tender plants of foreign countries kept alive by artificial heats, or withering in an air and soil that are not adapted to them.

Joseph Addison, *The Spectator*, 6 September 1712

GARDENS

A spaceship kitchen garden was provided for the cosmonauts who broke the world space endurance record with 211 days in the Soviet space station Salut-7 in 1982:

'I never before wanted to grow any plants, and for the first time in my life, I was taking care of a kitchen garden,' said Lebedev. He cultivated radishes, cucumbers and salad greens and said it was a psychological boost watching his space crops respond to 'a drop of water'.

Guardian, 7 January 1983

Plant life can be equally satisfying to those living in a confined urban environment:

> Ev'n in the stifling bosom of the town,
> A garden, in which nothing thrives, has charms
> That soothes the rich possessor; much consol'd,
> That here and there some sprigs of mournful mint,
> Or nightshade, or valerian, grace the well
> He cultivates ...
> What are the casements lin'd with creeping herbs,
> The prouder sashes fronted with a range
> Of orange, myrtle, or the fragrant weed,
> The Frenchman's darling? are they not all proofs
> That man, immur'd in cities, still retains
> His inborn inextinguishable thirst
> Of rural scenes, compensating his loss
> By supplemental shifts, the best he may?
> The most unfurnish'd with the means of life,
> And they that never pass their brick-wall bounds,
> To range the fields and treat their lungs with air,
> Yet feel the burning instinct: over head
> Suspend their crazy boxes, planted thick
> And water'd duly. There the pitcher stands
> A fragment, and the spoutless tea-pot there;
> Sad witnesses how close-pent man regrets
> The country, with what ardour he contrives
> A peep at Nature, when he can no more.

William Cowper, *The Task*, 1785

GARDENS AND GARDENERS

A fictional parapet garden on a London roof is owned by Tartar, a young naval lieutenant who offers to extend its delights for the benefit of Neville Landless who occupies the next door set of attic rooms:

'I have noticed... that you seem to like my garden aloft here. If you would like a little more of it, I could throw out a few lines and stays between my windows and yours, which the runners would take to directly. And I have some boxes, both of mignonette and wallflower, that I could shove on along the gutter (with a boat-hook I have by me) to your windows, and draw back again when they wanted watering or gardening, and shove on again when they were shipshape; so that they would cause you no trouble. I couldn't take this liberty without asking your permission, so I venture to ask it.'...

Neville replied that he was greatly obliged, and that he thankfully accepted the kind proposal.

Charles Dickens, *The Mystery of Edwin Drood*, 1870

A somewhat more elaborate rooftop garden, famed as a Wonder of the World, was created by one of the Assyrian Kings:

... having married a wife he was fond of, out of one of the provinces, where such paradises or gardens were much in use, and the country lady not well bearing the air or enclosure of the palace in Babylon to which the Assyrian kings used to confine themselves; he made her gardens, not only within the palaces, but upon terraces raised with earth, over the roofs, and even upon the top of the highest tower, planted them with all sorts of fruit-trees, as well as other plants and flowers, the most pleasant of that country; and there-by made at least the most airy gardens, as well as the most costly, that have been heard of in the world.

Sir William Temple, *Upon the Gardens of Epicurus*, 1685

GARDENS

The dedicated gardener will contrive an indoor garden too. Victorians were urged to enjoy the advantages of a window garden – a mini-greenhouse projecting from the window on iron brackets:

Another development of the enclosed window garden is that particular form which, some years ago, we designated the *hortus fenestralis*, the window garden *par excellence*, and the *multum in parvo* of its kind. It is an elegance peculiarly adapted for the window that commands an unpleasant look-out, or where inquisitive eyes impose a limit on privacy, or perhaps tongues that defy propriety make unseemly noises without. It is powerful to exclude noise, dust, and excess of light; and may be made a gratification to passers-by, as well as to those within the house, as may be desired.

Shirley Hibberd, Rustic Adornments for Homes of Taste, 1856

In a novel of the same century, Claude Mellot, an artist, entertains his friends in an indoor garden.

At the back, a glass bay has been thrown out, and forms a little conservatory, for ever fresh and gay with

GARDENS AND GARDENERS

tropic ferns and flowers; gaudy orchids dangle from the roof, creepers hide the framework, and you hardly see where the room ends and the winter-garden begins; and in the centre an ottoman invites you to lounge. It costs Claude money, doubtless; but he has his excuse – 'Having once seen the tropics, I cannot live without some love-tokens from their lost paradises; and which is the wiser plan, to spend money on a horse and brougham, which we don't care to use, and on scrambling into society at the price of one great stupid party a year, or to make our little world as pretty as we can, and let those who wish to see us, take us as they find us?'

Charles Kingsley, *Two Years Ago*, 1895

An old lady's cottage parlour shows that indoor gardening is not confined to town dwellers:

It was amazing. That she didn't find it so was clear from the start. Perhaps she thought everybody grew mind-your-own-business in old shell cases from the Western Front. Perhaps she thought every house had it frothing all over the clock and the ornaments, and climbing down the mantel towards the scuttle... Miss Murry lifted a dense curtain of its bubbly little leaves to have a look at the clock. I sat in a chair which seemed to have taken, for leaves pressed through its stretchers. Soft vermilion bells fell from their fragile stalks with every breath I took and the whole room smelled of fuchsias and spicy geraniums. Miss Murry sidled about getting tea. There was just enough room for her, her guest and the cake. The rest was botany.

Ronald Blythe, in *A Book of Gardens*, 1963

A well-grown window sill plant such as Campanula isophylla *can be an alluring sight, though it is not always wise to admire it too closely.*

The open saucer-shaped bells in white or violet blue, cover the plant in an almost solid cascade of bloom. I

GARDENS

was once admiring a particularly fine specimen in a cottage window with my friend Clarence Elliott, and speculating about the chances of a deal with its owner, when, our noses pressed against the glass in our enthusiasm, we became aware of a duplicate cascade behind that of the plant, and encountered the stony glare of a bearded cottager.

John Nash, in *The Saturday Book*, 1957

The thought of an indoor garden is never more beguiling than in winter, when outdoors all is hidden by a blanket of snow. The gardener, impatiently waiting for spring, throws himself down

on a sofa, couch, or settee, and tries to imitate the winter sleep of Nature.

In half an hour he flies up from this horizontal position, inspired by a new idea. Flower-pots! Aren't flowers grown in pots? At once thickets of palms, latanias, dracaenas, and tradescantias, asparagus, clivias, and begonias, in all their tropical beauty, rise before his eyes; and among them, of course, a forced primula, and hyacinth, and cyclamen will flower; in the corridor we shall make an equatorial jungle, hanging tendrils will flow from the stairs, and in the windows we shall put plants which will flower like mad. Then he glances quickly round; no longer does he see the room in which he lives, but a forest of paradise which he will create here, and he runs to the gardener at the corner to bring home an armful of the treasures of vegetation.

When he brings home as much as he can carry he finds:

That when he puts it all together it does not look at all like an equatorial forest, but rather like a small crockery shop;

That he can't put anything in the windows because – as the silly women at home declare – windows are for ventilation;

That he can't put anything on the stairs because it

would make them filthy with mud and splashed with water;

That he can't change the hall into a tropical forest because, in spite of his fervent entreaties and cursings, the women persist in opening the windows to the frosty air.

So he carries his treasures into the cellar, where, at least, as he comforts himself, it does not freeze; and in spring, poking in the warm soil outside, he forgets them completely. But this experience will by no means deter him next December from trying again with new flower-pots to transform his lodging into a winter garden. In it you see the eternal life of Nature.

Karel Čapek, *The Gardener's Year*, 1929

Gardening

It is not graceful, and it makes one hot; but it is a blessed sort of work, and if Eve had had a spade in Paradise and known what to do with it, we should not have had all that sad business of the apple.

> Countess von Arnim, *Elizabeth and Her German Garden*, 1898

... a labour full of tranquillity and satisfaction; natural and instructive, and such as (if any) contributes to the most serious contemplation, experience, health, and longevity ...

> John Evelyn, *Kalendarium Hortense*, 1666 (1706 ed.)

It tends to turn the minds of youth from amusements and attachments of a frivolous or vicious nature: it is a taste which is indulged at home: it tends to make home pleasant, and to endear us to the spot on which it is our lot to live: and, as to the expenses attending it, what are all these expenses, compared with those of the short, the unsatisfactory, the injurious enjoyments of the card-table, and the rest of those amusements or pastimes which are sought for in the town?

> William Cobbett, *The English Gardener*, 1829

Those of us who enjoy gardening agree wholeheartedly with such sentiments, but others are puzzled by our enthusiasm:

And what an interest there has been lately in the popularity of gardening! A butler remarked recently that he didn't know what things were coming to. 'At one time,' he said, 'if you kept your ears open at a dinner party you could pick up a useful racing tip now and then; but all you hear nowadays is about the latest rhododendron or something, and the best manure to give it.'

C. H. Middleton, in *The Queen's Book of the Red Cross*, 1939

and some are downright antagonistic:

I have a strong antipathy to everything connected with gardens, gardening and gardeners... Gardening seems to me a kind of admission of defeat... Man was made for better things than pruning his rose trees. The state of mind of the confirmed gardener seems to me as reprehensible as that of the confirmed alcoholic. Both have capitulated to the world. Both have become lotus eaters and drifters.

Colin Wilson, in *A Book of Gardens*, 1963

Monstrous as this opinion is, the most dedicated gardener has to admit that gardening

has its snares, of which the chief is that it may become too interesting and too absorbing. Its very innocence may help on and even conceal the snare; but the snare is there as it is in everything else in this world, however good, and I never think of it without remembering Newman's striking poem on Jonah... which commences with the beautiful yet almost stern stanzas...

>Deep in his meditative bower,
> The tranquil seer reclined,
>Numbering the creepers of an hour,
> The gourds which o'er him twined.

GARDENING

> To note each plant, to rear each fruit
> Which soothes the languid sense;
> He deemed a safe, refined pursuit –
> His Lord, an indolence.
>
> – Lyra Apostolica, 'Jonah'
>
> Canon Ellacombe, *In a Gloucestershire Garden*, 1895

Aware of the pitfalls, however, we are not necessarily repentant.

There are times when I begin to wonder if I am not *too* devoted to my garden, *too* impatient of interruptions, *too* content doing some perhaps quite inessential garden job, with my husband not far away, busy hand-weeding, my beloved pug dog beside me, and my favourite robin sitting expectantly on a neighbouring twig. But I do not really think I want to be any different.

Valerie Finnis, in *A Gardener's Dozen*, 1980

Gardening was no mere hobby for these energetic nineteenth-century cottagers:

Two new cottages of a very superior character were erected in the corner of an arable field, abutting on the highway. As left by the builders a more uninviting spot could scarcely be imagined. The cottages themselves were well designed and well built, but the surroundings were like a wilderness. Heaps of rubbish here, broken bricks there, the ground trampled hard as the road itself. No partition from the ploughed field behind beyond a mere shallow trench enclosing what was supposed to be the garden. Everything bleak, unpromising, cold, and unpleasant. Two families went into these cottages, the men working on the adjoining farm. The aspect of the place immediately began to change. The rubbish was removed, the best of it going to improve the paths and approaches; a quickset hedge was planted round the enclosure. Evening after evening, be the weather what it might, these two men were in that garden at work – after a long day in the fields. In the dinner hour even they sometimes snatched a few minutes to trim something. Their spades turned over the whole of the soil, and planting commenced. Plots were laid out for cabbage, plots for potatoes, onions, parsnips.

Then having provided necessaries for the immediate future they set about preparing for extras. Fruit trees – apple, plum and damson – were planted; also some roses. Next beehives appeared and were elevated on stands and duly protected from the rain. The last work was the building of pigsties – rude indeed and made of a few slabs – but sufficient to answer the purpose. Flowers in pots appeared in the windows, flowers appeared beside the garden paths. The change was so complete and so quickly effected I could hardly realise that so short a time since there had been nothing there but a blank open space. Persons travelling along the road could not choose but look on and admire the transformation.

I had often been struck with the flourishing appearance of cottage gardens, but then those gardens were of old date and had reached that perfection in course of years. But here the thing seemed to grow up under one's eyes. All was effected by sheer energy. Instead of spending their evenings wastefully at 'public', these men went out into their gardens and made what was a desert literally bloom.

Richard Jefferies, *Hodge and His Masters*, 1880

Gardening has long been advocated as a thoroughly healthy activity.

Toil and be strong. By toil the flaccid nerves
Grow firm, and gain a more compacted tone...
                       Some love the manly foils;
The tennis some; and some the graceful dance;
Others, more hardy, range the purple heath
Or naked stubble; where from field to field
The sounding coveys urge their labouring flight;

GARDENING

Eager amid the rising cloud to pour
The gun's unerring thunder: and there are
Whom still the meed of the green archer charms.
But if through genuine tenderness of heart,
Or secret want of relish for the game,
You shun the glories of the chase, nor care
To haunt the peopled stream, the garden yields
A soft amusement, a humane delight.
To raise the insipid nature of the ground,
Or tame its savage genius to the grace
Of careless sweet rusticity, that seems
The amiable result of happy chance,
Is to create, and give a godly joy,
Which every year improves. Nor thou disdain
To check the lawless riot of the trees,
To plant the grove, or turn the barren mould.

John Armstrong, *The Art of Preserving Health*, 1744

I love chopping, sawing, digging, cutting, laying swathes of nettles with the scythe, breaking twigs for kindling or hoisting branches on to a pile. There is a delight in doing it, satisfaction when it is done, and pleasure afterwards in an easy chair with feet up and a glass of elderberry wine. The rhythm of the thing is important, that it should be done by hand, at the body's pace: I hate having to use machines in the garden.

Michael Dower, 'Living with a Garden', from *The Countryman*, Summer 1974

This bodily rhythm is echoed in the rhythm of the gardener's seasonal work.

A gardener's work is never at an end; it begins with the year, and continues to the next: he prepares the ground, and then he sows it; after that he plants, and then he gathers the fruits...

John Evelyn, *Kalendarium Hortense*, 1666 (1706 ed.)

The soil is prepared:

> Labour within your garden square
> Till back be broke and light grow rare,
> But never heed the sinew's pain
> If you may snatch before the rain
> Crisp days when clods will turn up rough;
> Gentleman robin brown as snuff
> With spindle legs and bright round eye
> Shall be your autumn company.
> Trench deep; dig in the rotting weeds;
> Slash down the thistle's greybeard seeds;
> Then make the frost your servant; make
> His million fingers pry and break
> The clods by glittering midnight stealth
> Into the necessary tilth.

V. Sackville-West, from *The Land*, 1927

The operation of digging ... is, however, a fine healthy occupation not only from its calling the muscles into vigorous action, but from the smell of the new earth being particularly invigorating; and you might have a lady's spade, with a smooth willow handle, that will enable you to dig a small bed without much difficulty.

Jane Loudon, *The Lady's Country Companion or How to Enjoy a Country Life Rationally*, 1845

there is nothing quite like that first, warmly moist smell of newly dug earth in spring; no sight that can quicken the heart like that newly turned bed ... For we have a kinship with the soil. That is why the elementary tasks in the garden – digging, sowing, raking – are so deeply satisfying. That is why mechanical aids to soil culture, however efficient they may be, never give the same feeling of satisfaction. The machine does the work, but there is no sympathy.

H. L. V. Fletcher, *Purest Pleasure*, 1948

The garden – or cultivated soil, also called humus, or mould – consists mainly of special ingredients, such as

GARDENING

earth, manure, leafmould, peat, stones, pieces of glass, mugs, broken dishes, nails, wire, bones, Hussite arrows, silver paper from slabs of chocolate, bricks, old coins, old pipes, plate-glass, tiny mirrors, old labels, tins, bits of string, buttons, soles, dog droppings, coal, pot-handles, wash-basins, dishcloths, bottles, sleepers, milkcans, buckles, horseshoes, jam tins, insulating material, scraps of newspapers, and innumerable other components which the astonished gardener digs up at every stirring of his beds.

Karel Čapek, The Gardener's Year, 1929

The provident gardener then provides himself with

A paper book to note what when and where he sows
and plants, and register the success of trials.

John Evelyn, Directions for the Gardiner at Says-
Court, 1686

and seeds are sown:

In March and in April, from morning to night:
in sowing and setting, good huswives delight.
To have in their garden or some other plot:
to trim up their house, and to furnish their pot.

Thomas Tusser, A Hundred Good Points of
Husbandry, 1557

Cucumber seed is sown in the hotbed:

The seed, selected wisely, plump, and smooth,
And glossy, he commits to pots of size
Diminutive, well fill'd with well-prepar'd
And fruitful soil, that has been treasur'd long,
And drank no moisture from the dripping clouds:
These on the warm and genial earth, that hides
The smoking manure and o'erspreads it all,
He places lightly, and, as time subdues
The rage of fermentation, plunges deep
In the soft medium, till they stand immers'd.
Then rise the tender germs, upstarting quick,
And spreading wide their spongy lobes ...

Two leaves produc'd, two rough indented leaves,
Cautious he pinches from the second stalk
A pimple, that portends a future sprout,
And interdicts its growth. Thence straight succeed
The branches, sturdy to his utmost wish;
Prolific all, and harbingers of more.
The crowded roots demand enlargement now,
And transplantation in an ampler space.
Indulg'd in what they wish, they soon supply
Large foliage, overshadowing golden flowers,
Blown on the summit of th'apparent fruit.

William Cowper, *The Task*, 1785

My neighbour...does the oddest things...She has not many real wooden seed boxes. There are cardboard dress-boxes tied round with string to prevent them from disintegrating, and old Golden Syrup tins, and even some of those tall tins that once contained Slug-death, and some of those little square chip-baskets called punnets. I verily believe that she would use an old shoe if it came handy. In this curious assortment of receptacles an equally curious assortment of seedlings are coming up, green as a lawn, prolific as mustard-and-cress on a child's bit of flannel. There are cabbages and lettuces in some of them; rare lilies in others; and I noted a terrified little crop of auriculas scurrying up, as though afraid that they might be late for a pricking-out into the warm earth of May.

It all goes to show what you can do if you try, in gardening. There are such possibilities, not necessarily expensive.

V. Sackville-West, *In Your Garden*, 1951

The year advances and the plot must be watered:

You shall seldom see a cottage hereabout without an accompanying pond, all alive with geese and ducks, at the end of the little garden. Ah! here is Dame Simmons making a most original use of her piece of water, standing on the bank that divides it from her garden, and most ingeniously watering her onion-bed with a new mop – now a dip, and now a twirl! Really, I give her credit for the invention. It is as good an imitation of a shower as one should wish to see on a summer day. A squirt is nothing to it!

Mary Russell Mitford, *Our Village*, 1824–32

There be some which use to water their beds with great squirts, made of tin, in drawing up the water, and setting the squirt to the breast, that by force squirted upward, the water in the breaking may fall as drops of rain on the plants, which sundry times like squirted on the beds, doth sufficiently feed the plants with moisture.

Thomas Hyll, *The Gardener's Labyrinth*, 1577

With a hydrant and hose, of course, one can water faster and, so to speak, wholesale; in a relatively short time we have watered not only the beds, but the lawn as well, the neighbour's family at their tea, the passers-by, the inside of the house, all the members of the family, and ourselves most of all. Such a jet from the hydrant has terriffic efficacy, almost like a machine-gun; in a jiffy you can drill with it a trench in the earth, mow down the perennials, and wrench crowns from the trees. It refreshes you enormously if you squirt with the nozzle against the wind ... A hose has also a special predilection for developing a hole somewhere in

GARDENS AND GARDENERS

the middle, where you expect it least; and then you are standing like a god of water in the midst of sparkling jets with a long snake coiled at your feet; it is an overwhelming sight. When you are wet to the skin you contentedly declare that the garden has had enough, and you go to get dry. In the meantime the garden said 'Ouf', lapped up your water without a wink, and is as dry and thirsty as it was before.

Karel Čapek, *The Gardener's Year*, 1929

Soil must be tilled, and plants tended:

On light evenings, after their tea-supper, the men worked for an hour or two in their gardens or on the allotments. They were first-class gardeners and it was their pride to have the earliest and best of the different kinds of vegetables. They were helped in this by good soil and plenty of manure from their pigsties; but good tilling also played its part. They considered keeping the soil constantly stirred about the roots of growing things the secret of success and used the Dutch hoe a good deal for this purpose. The process was called 'tickling'. 'Tickle up old Mother Earth and make her bear!' they would shout to each other across the plots, or salute a busy neighbour in passing with: 'Just tickling her up a bit, Jack?'

Flora Thompson, *Lark Rise to Candleford*, 1939

May 15 Thursday. A coldish dull morning – hoed the first row of peas, weeded etc....
Friday morning (16th) Warm and mild, after a fine night of rain. Transplanted radishes after breakfast...
June – Wednesday (4th)... In the Evening I was watering plants when Mr and Mrs Simpson called. I accompanied them home, and we went to the waterfall at the head of the valley... I brought home lemon thyme and several other plants, and planted them by moonlight.

Dorothy Wordsworth, *Journal*, 1800

GARDENING

GARDENING POEM

> 8 a.m. and the beans are ready for inspection
> No blackfly, no dingy leaves, all's well.
> The sun moves on, the shadows wheel,
> The garden, like a clock-face, tells the time
> Strawberries stand at ten,
> Sweet-corn at eleven, roses punctuate the day
> You dig potatoes, weed the radishes,
> Cut mint, bind honeysuckle.
> This is your platoon, your ward, your parish,
> In an election they would vote for you.
> Always, by God, you tend your troops
> Before seeking your own quarters,
> Watering them, bedding them down.
> They'll honour you; love pollinates
> All that it touches. Your hands are diligent
> Your fingers pinch, pluck, curry, and groom
> This year, the yield will be heavy. Harvest
> You say, begins at home.

Philip Oakes, *Selected Poems*, 1982

To a gardener, the weather is rarely ideal – either too cold:

I went to Say[e]s-Court to see how the frost and rigorous weather had dealt with my garden, where I found many of the greens and rare plants utterly destroyed; the oranges and myrtles very sick, the rosemary and laurel dead to all appearance, but the cypress like to endure it.

John Evelyn, *Diary*, 4 February 1684

June 7. Ice thick as a crown piece. Potatoes much injured, and whole rows of kidney-beans killed: nasturtiums killed.

Gilbert White, *Naturalist's Journal*, 1787

or too hot:

July 23. – Hot dry weather still. No rain coming we

were forced to put-out more annuals in the dusty border; to shade 'em well, and to give them a vast quantity of water. The garden looks quite destitute of crops: no turnips will come up; no celery can be trenched, nor endives, nor savoys planted out. The ponds in most parishes are quite dried up.

Gilbert White, *Garden Kalendar*, 1765

or so stormy that May optimism turns to July gloom:

May – Friday 28th ... In the garden we have lilies and many other flowers. The scarlet Beans are up in crowds. It is now between 8 and nine o'clock. It has rained sweetly for two hours and a half – the air is very mild. The heckberry blossoms are dropping off fast, almost gone – barberries are in beauty – snowballs coming forward – May roses blossoming.

Monday 4 July ... The Roses in the garden are fretted and battered and quite spoiled the honeysuckle though in its glory is sadly teazed. The peas are beaten down. The Scarlet Beans want sticking. The garden is overrun with weeds.

Dorothy Wordsworth, *Journal*, 1802

GARDENING

Those weeds are an ever-present problem:

> All hate the rank society of weeds,
> Noisome, and ever greedy to exhaust
> Th'impov'rish'd earth; an overbearing race,
> That, like the multitude made faction-mad,
> Disturb good order, and degrade true worth.
>
> William Cowper, *The Task*, 1785

Above all, be careful not to suffer weeds (especially nettles, dandelion, groundsel, and all downy-plants) to run up to seed; for they will in a moment infect the whole ground: wherefore, whatever work you neglect, ply weeding at the first peeping of ye Spring... Note that whilst the gardener rolls or mows, the weeder is to sweep and cleanse in the same method, and never to be taken from that work 'til she have finished: first the gravel walks and flower-borders; then the kitchen-gardens; to go over all this she is allowed one month every three-months, with the gardeners assistance of the haw, and rough digging; where curious hand-weeding is less necessary.

> John Evelyn, *Directions for the Gardiner at Says-Court*, 1686

At Woburn such humble work did not go unnoticed, for in the cherry garden there stood

a figure of stone resembling an old weeder woman used in the garden, and my Lord would have her effigy which is done so like and her clothes so well that at first I took it to be a real living body...

> *The Journeys of Celia Fiennes*, 1697

Gilbert White's handyman-gardener Thomas seems to have been something of a misogynist, though Goody Hampton the weeding woman met with his approval.

I am now going to retain my weeding woman for the summer. This is the person that Thomas says he likes as well as a man: and indeed excepting that she wears petticoats, and now and then has a child, you would think her a man. To the care and abilities of this Lady I shall entrust my garden, that it may be neat and tidy when you come.

Gilbert White, letter to his niece Molly, 13 April 1778

Along with weeds come pests:

Weeds are always growing, the great mother of all living creatures, the earth, is full of seed in her bowels, and any stirring gives them heat of sun, and being laid near day, they grow: moles work daily, though not always alike...

William Lawson, A New Orchard and Garden, 1618

Many there be, which to drive away these harmful moles, do bring up young cats in their garden ground, and make tame weasels, to the end that either of these, through the hunting after them, may so drive away this pestiferous annoyance, being taught to watch at their straight passages and mouths of the holes...

Thomas Hyll, The Gardener's Labyrinth, 1577

MOLE-TRAP

> When we arrived the trap was empty.
> An hour later, after we had talked
> And admired the view, we walked
> On the lawn and found him lying limply,
> A fat prelatical mole
> With pudgy pink hands.
> While we were chatting politely, his sands
> Had run out. His velvet was cool
> Already to touch. He was a nuisance,
> Spoiling the lawn with his heaps of earth,
> Unlicensed upheavals like the birth
> Of garden volcanoes. Sentence
> Of death had to be passed, no doubt,
> And had been carried out.
> It was sentimental to regret
> That clerical-looking rogue. And yet...

Ruth Bidgood, in The Countryman, Winter 1968

Poultry and cats are to be hindered from scraping and basking by laying brambles, and holly-bushes on the beds.

John Evelyn, *Directions for the Gardiner at Says-Court*, 1686

At Clifford Priory, Radnorshire:

We wandered up into the twilit garden and there among the strawberries fastened to a little kennel by a collar and a light chain to keep the birds away was a most dear delightful white pussy ...

Revd Francis Kilvert, *Diary*, 9 July 1870

The coleworts and all pot herbs are greatly defended from the gnawing of the garden fleas, by radish growing among them.

Thomas Hyll, *The Gardener's Labyrinth*, 1577

May 31. – Sowed a pint more of large French-beans. The first sowings strangely devoured by snails.

Septem^r. 8. – The wasps (which are without number this dry hot summer) attack the grapes in a grievous manner. Hung-up 16 bottles with treacle, and beer, which make great havoc among them.

Octr. 18. – Hares or some vermin have gnawed almost all the fine pheasant-eyed pinks, and the new-planted cabbages.

Gilbert White, *Garden Kalendar*, 1759, 1762, 1763

Larger animals can be equally troublesome:

M d'Arblay has worked most laboriously in his garden, but his misfortunes there, during our absence, might melt a heart of stone. The horses of our neighbouring farmer broke through our hedges, and have made a kind of bog of our meadow, by scampering in it during the wet; the sheep followed, who have eaten up all our greens, every sprout and cabbage and lettuce destined for the winter, while the horses dug up our turnips and carrots; and the swine, pursuing such examples, have trod down all the young plants, besides devouring whatever the others left of vegetables.

Fanny Burney, *Diary and Letters of Madame d'Arblay*, 1800

There are human pests too:

Septr. 18. – In the night between the 16: and 17: my melons and cucumbers were pulled all to pieces; and the horse-block, three hand glasses, and many other things were destroyed by persons unknown.

Gilbert White, *Garden Kalendar*, 1764

Half a dozen flowers were cropped on May-morning, but the offenders have been detected, and brought to open shame. And this, considering ye numbers, that pay their compliments to ye place on Sunday-evenings, is a small infringement, scarce worth mentioning.

William Shenstone, letter to Lady Luxborough, 14 May 1749

Such phlegmatism is enviable. Here a more choleric gardener is roused into aggressive action, when his gullible wife Euphemia is attracted by the horticultural marvels offered by a persistent doorstep salesman. The family dog, having chased the caller up a tree, is restrained, and the man descends nervously:

'If you will just tie up that dog, sir,' said the agent, 'and come this way, I would like to show you the Meltinagua pear – dissolves in the mouth like snow, sir; trees will bear next year.'

'Oh, come look at the Royal Sparkling Ruby grape!' cried Euphemia. 'It glows in the sun like a gem.'

'Yes,' said the agent, 'and fills the air with fragrance during the whole month of September –'

'I tell you,' I shouted, 'I can't hold this dog another minute! The chain is cutting the skin off my hands. Run, sir, run! I'm going to let go!'

The agent now began to be frightened, and shut up his book.

'If only you could see the plates, sir, I'm sure –'

'Are you ready?' I cried, as the dog... made a bolt in his direction.

'Good-day, if I must –' said the agent, as he hurried to the gate. But there he stopped.

'There is nothing, sir,' he said, 'that would so improve your place as a row of the Spitzenburg Sweet-scented Balsam fir along this fence. I'll sell you three-year-old trees –'

'He's loose!' I shouted, as I dropped the chain.

In a second the agent was on the other side of the gate.

Frank R. Stockton, *Rudder Grange*, 1883

The Five Senses

I enjoy the use of all five senses. The look of a garden can be a great joy – the massing of trees and shrubs, the stretch of lawn, the detailed beauty of a flower, reflections in water and the dappling of shadows – but the other senses also should bring delight. I value the smells that come from working in the garden – bruised elder-twigs, the sawdust of apple-wood, cut logs of the bay-tree, fungus, damp earth and bonfires. I value also the taste of things picked and eaten at once, such as water-cress and blackberries; the feel of bark, of cool snowdrop stems in the picking, of hot rough stones in the sun, of water when cleaning the spade; and, of course, the sounds of the garden – birds calling, house martins twittering as they swoop from the eaves of the house, bees humming up the full height of a flower-covered lime tree, a hen clucking after laying an egg, water falling into the pond. But most of all, the sound of the wind, soft through the leaves and sometimes roaring through the branches as through the rigging of a tall ship in a storm.

Michael Dower, in *The Countryman*, Summer 1974

THE FIVE SENSES

The life of man in this world is but a thraldom, when the senses are not pleased; and what rarer object can there be on earth... than a beautiful and odiferous garden plat artificially composed, where he may read and contemplate on the wonderful works of the great Creator, in plants and flowers; for if he observeth with a judicial eye, and a serious judgement their variety of colours, scents, beauty, shapes, interlacing, enamelling, mixture, turnings, windings, embossments, operations and virtues, it is most admirable to behold, and meditate upon the same.

Thomas Hyll, *The Gardener's Labyrinth*, 1577

Who would look dangerously up at planets that might safely look down at plants?

John Gerard, *Herball*, 1597

The trees and shrubs are in full bloom, all of a sudden ... The servants are now very busy in clearing my grove etc.; whither I stray now, two or three times a day, with great complacency.

William Shenstone, letter to Lady Luxborough, 24 May 1751

After any enforced separation from his plants the keen gardener rushes into the garden to see how they have fared in his absence:

There are certain very definite rules to be observed when you are Making The Tour. The chief rule is that you must never take anything out of its order. You may be longing to see if a crocus has come out in the orchard, but it is strictly forbidden to look before you have inspected all the various beds, bushes and trees that lead up to the orchard.

You must not look at the bed ahead before you have finished with the bed immediately in front of you. You may see, out of the corner of your eye, a gleam of strange and unsuspected scarlet in the next bed but one, but you must steel yourself against rushing to this exciting blaze, and you must stare with cool eyes at the earth in front, which is apparently blank, until you have made certain that it is not hiding anything. Otherwise you will find that you rush wildly round the garden, discover one or two sensational events, and then decide that nothing else has happened. Which means that you miss all the thrill of tiny shoots, the first lifting of the lids of the wall flowers, the first precious gold of the witch-hazel, the early spear of the snowdrop.

Beverley Nichols, *Down the Garden Path*, 1932

More visual delights:

The vernal crocus or saffron flowers of the Spring, white, purple, yellow and striped, with some vernal colchicum or meadow saffron among them, some *Dens Caninus* or dog's teeth, and some of the small early leucojum or bulbous violet, all planted in some proportion as near one unto another as is fit for them, will give such a grace to the garden, that the place will seem like a piece of tapestry of many glorious colours, to increase everyone's delight ...

John Parkinson, *Paradisi in Sole Paradisus Terrestris*, 1597

'Do bulbs live a long time? ...' inquired Mary anxiously.

'They're things as helps themselves,' said Martha. 'That's why poor folks can afford to have them. If you don't trouble 'em, most of 'em'll work away underground for a lifetime an' spread out an' have little 'uns. There's a place in th' park woods here where there's snowdrops by thousands. They're the prettiest sight in Yorkshire when th' spring comes.'

Frances Hodgson Burnett, *The Secret Garden*, 1911

> Soon will the high Midsummer pomps come on,
>   Soon will the musk carnations break and swell,
> Soon shall we have gold-dusted snapdragon,
>   Sweet-William with his homely cottage-smell,
>   And stocks in fragrant blow;

> Roses that down the alleys shine afar,
>   And open, jasmine-muffled lattices,
>   And groups under the dreaming garden-trees,
> And the full moon, and the white evening-star.
>
> Matthew Arnold, *Thyrsis*, 1866

the stocks held open their fresh plump purses, of a pink as fragrant and as faded as old Spanish leather...

Marcel Proust, *Swann's Way*, 1922

Flowers of the Sun groweth very high, and beareth a great yellow flower as big as the crown of a hat...

Thomas Hyll, *The Gardener's Labyrinth*, 1577

there are many kinds of roses, differing either in the bigness of the flowers, or the plant itself, roughness or smoothness, or in the multitude or fewness of the flowers, or else in colour and smell; for divers of them are high and tall, others short and low, some have five leaves, others very many. Moreover, some be red, others white, and most of them or all sweetly smelling, especially those of the garden.

John Gerard, *Herball*, 1597

In the good days when nothing in Woolworth's cost over sixpence, one of their best lines was their rose bushes. They were always very young plants, but they came into bloom in their second year, and I don't think I ever had one die on me. Their chief interest was that they were never, or very seldom, what they claimed to be on their labels. One that I bought for a Dorothy Perkins turned out to be a beautiful little white rose with a yellow heart, one of the finest ramblers I have ever seen. A polyantha rose labelled yellow turned out to be deep red. Another, bought for an Albertine, was like an Albertine, but more double, and gave astonishing masses of blossom. These roses had all the interest of a surprise packet, and there was always the chance that you might happen upon a new variety which you would have the right to name John Smithii or something of that kind.

Last summer I passed the cottage where I used to live before the war. The little white rose, no bigger than a boy's catapult when I put it in, had grown into a huge vigorous bush, the Albertine or near-Albertine was smothering half the fence in a cloud of pink blossom. I had planted both of these in 1936. And I thought, 'All that for sixpence!' I do not know how long a rose bush lives; I suppose ten years might be an average life. And throughout that time a rambler will be in full bloom for a month or six weeks each year, while a bush rose will be blooming, on and off, for at least four months. All that for sixpence – the price, before the war, of ten Players, or a pint and a half of mild, or a week's subscription to the *Daily Mail*, or about twenty minutes of twice-breathed air in the movies!

George Orwell, *Tribune*, 21 January 1944

I have heard conventionally-minded people remark that they like a rose to be a rose, by which they apparently mean an overblown pink, scarlet, or yellow object, desirable enough in itself, but lacking the subtlety to be found in some of these traditional roses which might well be picked off a medieval tapestry or a piece of Stuart needlework. Indeed, I think you should approach them as though they were textiles rather than flowers. The velvet vermilion of petals, the stamens of quivering gold, the slaty purple of *Cardinal Richelieu*, the loose dark red and gold of *Alain Blanchard*; I could go on for ever, but always I should come back to the idea of embroidery and of velvet and of the damask with which some of them share their name.

V. Sackville-West, *In Your Garden*, 1951

And after all the weather was ideal. They could not have had a more perfect day for a garden party if they had ordered it. Windless, warm, the sky without a cloud. Only the blue was veiled with a haze of light

THE FIVE SENSES

Penshurst Place, Kent

gold, as it is sometimes in early summer. The gardener had been up since dawn, mowing the lawns and sweeping them, until the grass and the dark flat rosettes where the daisy plants had been seemed to shine. As for the roses, you could not help feeling they understood that roses are the only flowers that impress people at garden parties; the only flowers that anybody is certain of knowing. Hundreds, yes, literally hundreds had come out in a single night; the green bushes bowed down as though they had been visited by archangels.

Katherine Mansfield, The Garden Party, 1922

> And this is certain; if so be
> You could just now my garden see,
> The aspic of my flowers so bright
> Would make you shudder with delight.
>
> And if you voz to see my roziz
> As is a boon to all men's noziz, –
> You'd fall upon your back and scream –
> 'O Lawk! O criky! it's a dream!'

Edward Lear, postscript to a letter to Lord Carlingford, 30 April 1885

Such enthusiasm is fine in private, but voiced in public it can sometimes lead to embarrassment:

The danger the publication of ill-considered enthusiasm may lead to was very forcibly brought home to me when, long ago now, for a year or two I ran the gardening column in the *Sunday Times*. One October I had extolled the beauty of *Tulipa fosterana*... and recommended, with a journalist's gush, its immediate purchase and planting on a massive scale: 'If you can only afford a dozen, then buy a dozen. If you can afford a hundred, buy a hundred. But if you can afford a thousand, when May comes you will bless me.' I had myself bought, for my cat-run at Eton, half a dozen bulbs, one of which was to forget to put in an appearance. So I was not a little embarrassed when in the following spring the secretary of an Essex ladies' gardening club announced her intention of bringing two coachloads of its members to see my tulips at the height of their glory.

Wilfrid Blunt, in *A Gardener's Dozen*, 1980

Apart from flowers the garden holds other visual attractions:

Just think of the beauty that is available in leaves alone. We can use the big, fingered foliage of peonies, acanthus, anemones, filipendulas, astilbes and hellebores to offset the sword-like leaves of phormiums, the tall irises, the arching day lilies and the invaluable range of ornamental grasses. We can plant solid clumps of the bold, rounded leaves of bergenias, hostas and brunneras to contrast with the filigree of ferns. We can get untold satisfaction from the convoluted and scalloped glaucous grey of the seakale, the woolly grey of mullein and stachys, the silvery lace of absinthe.

Graham Stuart Thomas, *Perennial Garden Plants*, 1976

THE FIVE SENSES

As we admire the shapes of leaves we can enjoy their contrasting textures too:

there is a good tactile quality, like that of fine Morocco leather, in the dark, ribbed leaves of *Viburnum davidii*, a feeling of hard green wax in *Daphne laureola*; and of sculptured stone in the fluted, columnar stems of the common fennel. An evergreen bramble, *Rubus irenaeus*, is remarkable in a fierce race not only for its refinement, but for a combination of rigidity with peculiar softness in its large heart-shaped leaves, which have a faint metallic sheen on their upper surface. The great rosette of *Verbascum pannosum* is not only the whitest, I think, of the genus, but also the finest in texture, which is more like a delicate felt than the 'cloth', which its specific name implies. An opposite impression is given by the granite leaves of *Cyclamen neapolitanum* and by the young shoots of the spurge *Euphorbia sikkimensis*, which are almost glassy in their red translucency. *Sedum acre*... is hard and crumbly to the touch.

Jason Hill, *The Contemplative Gardener*, 1940

Vegetables too are decorative – a row of spinach

gone to seed, tangled in long whips of seed, half brown, half green as it ripens... looks like something from an Indian painting... There might be tigers here and the dying seed stems give the garden an oriental touch, just as the florets of leek seed on their tall sea-green stems look like pashas' hats.

James Turner, in *A Book of Gardens*, 1963

Certain potatoes, while not exactly decorative, can be visually impressive:

Everybody knew the elephant was an unsatisfactory potato, that it was awkward to handle when paring and that it boiled down to a white pulp in cooking; but it produced tubers of such astonishing size that none of the men could resist the temptation to plant it.

Every year specimens were taken to the inn to be weighed on the only pair of scales in the hamlet, then handed round for guesses to be made of the weight. As the men said, when a patch of elephants was dug up and spread out, 'You'd got summat to put in your eye and look at.'

Flora Thompson, *Lark Rise to Candleford*, 1939

A well-planned garden is visually satisfying in winter too:

Brown is a colour, even though it does not occur in the rainbow, and its warm quality makes it pleasant to the eye in winter, but although for many years I have admired the clear fawn of the fronds of bracken which have found a last refuge in the hedgebank (their winter colour once matched and hid the fallow deer) it occurred to me only recently that it might be combined with other fillimot [*sic*] shades into a brown garden for the winter prospect. There are several plants which turn and stay brown in winter and may be planted without the misgiving which the indomitable bracken may well occasion in the garden; that neglected little plant *Polygonum affine* provides a bright rust brown, montbretia and *Iris sibirica* a rich bay with snuff-coloured seed heads, henbane and teazel a pale silvery brown, *Cryptomeria japonica elegans* a cloudy bronze and the dwarf box, *Buxus microphylla*, a peculiar pinkish cinnamon. During the summer these appear to be an indiscriminate collection, but with the first frosts the harmony of their winter picture begins to develop.

Jason Hill, *The Contemplative Gardener*, 1940

I have often wondered that those who are like myself, and love to live in gardens, have never thought of contriving a Winter Garden, which should consist of such trees only as never cast their leaves. We have very often little snatches of sunshine and fair weather in the most uncomfortable parts of the year, and have frequently several days in November and January that

THE FIVE SENSES

are as agreeable as any in the finest months. At such times, therefore, I think there could not be a greater pleasure, than to walk in such a Winter Garden as I have proposed ... I have so far indulged myself in this thought, that I have set apart a whole acre of ground for the executing of it. The walls are covered with ivy instead of vines. The laurel, the hornbeam, and the holly, with many other trees and plants of the same nature, grow so thick in it, that you cannot imagine a more lively scene.

Joseph Addison, *The Spectator*, 6 September 1712

Fragrance is undoubtedly one of the greatest delights of the garden.

A man who makes a garden should have a heart for plants that have the gift of sweetness as well as beauty of form or colour.

William Robinson, *The English Flower Garden*, 1883

Gardens were more thought on at Caerhays than at Gorran. The Sargents and the Martins at the Hovel had gardens never without a bloom. A monthly rose bush in the Sargents' garden was one I particularly loved. Garden scents rather than wild scents lingered round Caerhays – lilies of the valley by the Martins' gate; moss-roses by the Sargents' gooseberry bushes; sweet violets or heliotrope under the Blandfords' wall; mignonette on either side of our own path; great tea roses over the Rectory veranda. All the land was more intensively cultivated than at Gorran; garden flowers grew even outside the gardens, but they were almost wild garden flowers, fragrant. The roses were not composed, scentless images, but full of nature, having the virtue of roses.

Anne Treneer, *School House in the Wind*, 1944

July-flowers, commonly called Gilly-flowers, or Clove July-flowers, (I call them so, because they flower in July) they have the name of cloves, of their scent. I may well call them the king of flowers except the rose, and the best sort of them are called Queen July-flowers. I have of them nine or ten several colours, and divers of them as big as roses; of all flowers (save the Damask Rose) they are the most pleasant to sight and smell ... their use is much in ornament, and comforting the spirits, by the sense of smelling.

William Lawson, *A New Orchard and Garden*, 1618

And because the breath of flowers is far sweeter in the air (where it comes and goes like the warbling of music) than in the hand, therefore nothing is more fit for that delight, than to know what be the flowers and plants that do best perfume the air. Roses, damask and red, are fast flowers of their smells; so that you may walk by a whole row of them, and find nothing of their sweetness; yea though it be in a morning's dew. Bays likewise yield no smell as they grow. Rosemary little; nor sweet marjoram. That which above all others yields the sweetest smell in the air, is the violet, specially the white double violet, which comes twice a year; about the middle of April, and about Bartholomew-tide. Next to that is the musk-rose. Then the strawberry-leaves dying, with a most excellent cordial smell. Then the flower of the vines; it is a little dust, like the dust of a bent, which grows upon the cluster in the first coming forth. Then sweet-briar. Then wallflowers, which are very delightful to be set under a parlour or lower chamber window. Then pinks and gilliflowers, specially the matted pink and clove gilliflower. Then the flowers of the lime-tree. Then the honeysuckles, so they be somewhat afar off. Of bean-flowers I speak not, because they are field flowers. But those which perfume the air most delightfully, not passed by as the rest, but being trodden upon and crushed, are three; that is, burnet, wild-thyme, and watermints. Therefore you are to set whole alleys of them, to have the pleasure when you walk or tread.

Francis Bacon, *Of Gardens*, 1625

THE FIVE SENSES

Recently I was staying with an old countryman in his tiny oak-beamed cottage, the rooms darkened by the scented-leaf geraniums which were in every window, and each evening on his return from his work in the fields he would take a full pint of cider and in silence and with a smack of his lips would say, whatever the weather: 'Well, are you ready?' That was the signal for which I had been waiting all day, for a walk in his old world garden before dusk. In spring we would enjoy a more delicate perfume, the sweet smell of broad beans in flower, of violets and primroses hiding amongst the new growth of the herbaceous plants for the garden was typical of the old world cottage, entirely without any order which made it all the more exciting. There would be daffodils in plenty and apple blossom, a few wallflowers growing as perennials and the leaves of rosemary, lavender and bay, in fact, all the plants known to Elizabethan gardens...

In late July, the perfumes would be stronger. There was the rich scent of the deep crimson roses and the powerful fragrance of the Madonna lilies and of stocks ... Then in autumn, the fragrance was more aromatic, more pungent, with the ripened herbs, the autumn fruiting raspberries and the dying strawberry leaves... And what fun those walks down his old garden were, seeking out flowers half hidden by a neighbouring plant, squeezing the leaves of others to make them give of their aromatic scent, popping into one's mouth a strawberry, or a fully ripened gooseberry, not the flavourless fruits of today, but those packed with fragrance, sweet and juicy like Black Prince strawberry and Red Champagne gooseberry. In late autumn my friend would say: 'Try that', pointing to a matured russet apple, possibly D'Arcy Spice, which looked so unattractive and misshapen, but its aroma and crispness upon eating made our handsome looking, imported apples eat like cotton wool. We would spend about an hour and then come in for tea or supper, depending upon the time of year. 'That's done me good', my friend would always say, whilst he lit the lamp or untied his boots...

> Roy Genders, *Perfume in the Garden*, 1955

Young Susan in the kitchen garden at Windystone Hall:

Waves of wormwood, rue, and fennel spread round her, sharpening her senses, clearing her head with their bitter smells. Marjoram and sage were homely kitchen scents, but these others cast a chill over her as she looked at their dull leaves.

> Alison Uttley, *The Country Child*, 1931

Another child enjoys aromatic foliage as she accompanies her father on a stroll through a greenhouse full of sweet-leaved geraniums:

No notice was taken of me, and so, left to my own devices, I would snip as I went, a leaf here, a leaf there, until finally with my hands and pockets full of aromatic leaves I would subside on an upturned tub in a corner and sniff and compare the different scents to my heart's content. It was a very good game indeed, as well as valuable nose training. It always seemed amazing that just leaves could have such a variety of odours. Some had the scents of oranges or lemons, some were spicy, others had a rose-like fragrance, and many were vaguely familiar but tantalizingly elusive. One that especially ravished my youthful nose smelled exactly like the pennyroyal that grew in our woods. The leaves of this kind were large and soft, and the bush was lax and ungainly in habit. I know it now for *Pelargonium tomentosum*, usually called the peppermint geranium. But my favourite was a little slender plant with small much-cut leaves that had the sharp refreshing scent of lemon, with something sweet behind it. It had the charm of lemon drops – acid and sweet – and always made my mouth water ecstatically. It was probably *P. citriodorum.*

L. B. Wilder quoted by Eleanour Sinclair Rohde in
The Scented Garden, 1931

Today I think
Only with scents, – scents dead leaves yield,
And bracken, and wild carrot's seed,
And the square mustard field.

Odours that rise
When the spade wounds the root of tree,
Rose, currant, raspberry, or goutweed,
Rhubarb or celery;

The smoke's smell, too,
Flowing from where a bonfire burns
The dead, the waste, the dangerous,
And all to sweetness turns.

It is enough
To smell, to crumble the dark earth,
While the robin sings over again
Sad songs of Autumn mirth.

Edward Thomas, *Collected Poems*, 1936

GARDENS AND GARDENERS

Some scents can be overpowering...

The flowers of the evergreen magnolia, and those of the orange, have an oppressive fragrance, as have those of the heliotrope and the tuberose...

Jane Loudon, *The Lady's Country Companion*, 1845

Our ginger plant is now in magnificent blossom, a curious tendrilled flower like an orchis, and the scent so strong that we have been obliged to turn the plant from the dining into the drawing room and thence into the hall.

Revd Francis Kilvert, *Diary*, 2 October 1874

Muscari: The dark blue Grape-flower... bearing at the top many small heavy bottle-like flowers... of a very strong smell, like unto starch when it is new made, and hot...
Sunflower: The whole plant, and every part thereof above ground hath a strong resinous scent of turpentine...

John Parkinson, *Paradisi in Sole Paradisus Terrestris*, 1597

... and other scents are downright unpleasant:

Phloxes smell to me like a combination of pepper and pig-stye, most brooms of dirty, soapy bath-sponge, hawthorn of fish-shop, and meadow-sweet of curry powder...

E. A. Bowles, *My Garden in Summer*, 1914

There is a curious smell about the yellow roots of berberis, not exactly nasty, and a strong odour, not really offensive, but that I personally dislike, about the root of *Chrysanthemum maximum*... The only other hardy flowers I can think of whose smell is distinctly offensive are *Lilium pyrenaicum*, smelling like a mangy dog, and some of the schizanthus, that are redolent of dirty hen-house.

Gertrude Jekyll, *Wood and Garden*, 1899

THE FIVE SENSES

One gardener neatly solved the difficulty of defining flower scents:

My one-time music teacher, Kenneth Stubbs, who was also an expert gardener, used to classify flower scents into those that are moral and those that are immoral. The distinction, when you come to think of it, is quite clear. Moral scents include all those warm, foody, daytime smells, like coconut-scented gorse, clove carnations, vanilla *Azara microphylla*, mignonette, lupins, wallflowers, stocks and thyme.

The immoral kind reserve their main strength, appropriately, for evening and night-time.

Christopher Lloyd, *The Well-Tempered Garden*, 1970

Probably the most powerfully seductive of all these evening treasures is

the small annual night-scented stock (*Matthiola bicornis*), a plant that in daytime is almost ugly; for the leaves are of a dull-grey colour, and the flowers are small and also dull-coloured, and they are closed and droop and look unhappy. But when the sun has set the modest little plant seems to come to life; the grey foliage is almost beautiful in its harmonious relation to the half-light; the flowers stand up and expand, and in the early twilight show tender colouring of faint pink and lilac, and pour out upon the still night-air a lavish gift of sweetest fragrance; and the modest little plant that in strong sunlight looked unworthy of a place in the garden, now rises to its appointed rank and reigns supreme as its prime delight.

Gertrude Jekyll, *Wood and Garden*, 1899

Some other evening scents, and sounds:

the clumps of white phlox seemed like bushes spread with linen; a moth ricochetted over them, and right across the garden... A few whiffs of the raw, strong scent of phlox invigorated her. She passed along the path, hesitating at the white rose-bush. It smelled sweet and simple. She touched the white ruffles of the roses. Their fresh scent and cool, soft leaves reminded her of the morning-time and sunshine.

D. H. Lawrence, *Sons and Lovers*, 1913

Somewhere in the vegetable patch they were watering cucumber beds, clanking the chain of the well as they drew the water and poured it from pail to pail.

There was a smell of all the flowers at once, as if the earth had been unconscious all day long and were now waking.

And from the Countess's centuries-old garden, so littered with fallen branches that it was impenetrable, the dusty aromatic smell of old lime trees coming into blossom drifted in a huge wave as tall as a house.

Boris Pasternak, *Doctor Zhivago*, 1958

Often, on moonlight nights in spring, the solitary fork of some one who had not been able to tear himself away would be heard and the scent of his twitch fire smoke would float in at the windows. It was pleasant, too, in summer twilight, perhaps in hot weather when water was scarce, to hear the *swish* of water on parched earth in a garden – water which had been fetched from the brook a quarter of a mile distant.

Flora Thompson, *Lark Rise to Candleford*, 1939

Rain, wind, and fire add their voices:

Come up to the first floor and look out of one of the windows over the tops of the yews and the flowering trees, through the great elms and into the wide upper Thames meadows. Winter and summer for three centuries while the Turner family lived here this stone grew lichened and from those water spouts the heavy rain fell on to the deep green grass of the garden from between the gables. Never did you hear such a noise of English wet as when the rain pours off Kelmscott Manor roof and splashes on to the grass and garden paths.

John Betjeman, in *The Best of Betjeman*, 1978

THE FIVE SENSES

The garden has something to offer not only to the eye; even the attentive ear is sometimes rewarded. We all know the patter of the 'rainy-sounding' leaves of the poplars when they are stirred by a light breeze and their imitation of a wave breaking on the shingle when they thresh the air on their long peduncles in a strong wind, but we are less appreciative than the Chinese of the delicate whisper of the bamboos, like the frou-frou of a silk petticoat that some of us are old enough to remember, nor do we commonly notice the dry rustle of a handful of alpine strawberries or of the bells of *Campanula caespitosa* and the common harebell. Yet all these sounds and others like them, have a pleasant timbre, which makes them worth listening to for their own sake and apart from their meaning and associations.

Jason Hill, *The Contemplative Gardener*, 1940

... bonfires that roar and crackle like dragons and can be kept in for a whole weekend with care and skill and the right weather and which finally smoulder more and more slowly, and putter out in a soft sigh of ash.

Susan Hill, *The Magic Apple Tree*, 1982

Pleasures & Pursuits

I asked a schoolboy, in the sweet summertide, 'what he thought a garden was for?' and he said, *Strawberries*. His younger sister suggested *Croquet*, and the elder *Garden-parties*. The brother from Oxford made a prompt declaration in favour of *Lawn Tennis and Cigarettes*, but he was rebuked by a solemn senior, who wore spectacles, and more back hair than is usual with males, and was told that 'a garden was designed for botanical research, and for the classification of plants'. He was about to demonstrate the differences between the *Acoty-* and the *Monocoty-ledonous* divisions, when the collegian remembered an engagement elsewhere.

I repeated my question to a middle-aged nymph, who wore a feathered hat of noble proportions over a loose green tunic with a silver belt, and she replied, with a rapturous disdain of the ignorance which presumed to ask – 'What is a garden for? For the soul, sir, for the soul of the poet! For visions of the invisible, for grasping the intangible, for hearing the inaudible, for exaltations above the miserable dullness of common life into the splendid regions of imagination and romance.'... A capacious gentleman informed me that nothing in horticulture touched him so sensibly as green peas and new potatoes, and he spoke with so much cheerful candour that I could not get angry; but my indignation was roused by a morose millionaire, when he declared that of all his expenses he grudged most the outlay on his confounded garden.

Dean Hole, Our Gardens, 1899

There must be amusements in every family. Children observe and follow their parents in almost every thing. How much better, during a long and dreary winter, for daughters, and even sons, to assist, or attend, their mother, in a green-house, than to be seated with her at cards, or, in the blubberings over a stupid novel, or at any other amusement that can possibly be conceived!

William Cobbett, *The English Gardener*, 1829

The creator of the Biggles flying stories, a keen gardener in retirement, had an unconventional solution for world peace:

if everyone was given a greenhouse at birth he wouldn't dare to leave it for fear of the fire going out, and that would put an end to war.

Captain W. E. Johns, *My Garden*, March 1940

William Cowper said of his greenhouse and garden, 'I am proud of neither, except in poetry, because there I can fib without lying, and represent them better than they are.' Here is the greenhouse in verse:

> Who loves a garden loves a green-house too,
> Unconscious of a less propitious clime,
> There blooms exotic beauty, warm and snug,
> While the winds whistle and the snows descend.

The spiry myrtle with unwith'ring leaf
Shines there, and flourishes. The golden boast
Of Portugal and western India there,
The ruddier orange, and the paler lime,
Peep through their polish'd foliage at the storm,
And seem to smile at what they need not fear.
Th'amomum there with intermingling flow'rs
And cherries hangs her twigs. Geranium boasts
Her crimson honours, and the spangled beau,
Ficoides, glitters bright the winter long.
All plants, of ev'ry leaf, that can endure
The winter's frown, if screen'd from his shrewd bite,
Live there, and prosper.

William Cowper, *The Task*, 1785

And here is the greenhouse in reality, described to 'dear Cuzzy-Wuzzy', Cowper's cousin Harriet:

My dear, I will not let you come till the end of May or beginning of June, because before that time my greenhouse will not be ready to receive us, and it is the only pleasant room belonging to us. When the plants go out we go in. I line it with mats, and spread the floor with mats; and there you shall sit with a bed of mignonette at your side, and a hedge of honeysuckles, roses, and jasmine; and I will make you a bouquet of myrtle every day.

William Cowper, letter to Lady Hesketh, 9 February 1786

In their devotion to plants some enthusiasts will go to great lengths, as this visitor to a deprived family discovered:

While conversing with the wife of a mechanic during the coldest period of a recent winter, she observed that the parental bed appeared to be scantily and insufficiently clothed, and she inquired if there were no more blankets in the house. 'Yes, ma'am, we've another,' replied the housewife; 'but –' and here she paused.

'But what?' said the lady.

'It is not at home, ma'am.'

'Surely, surely it's not in pawn?'

'Oh dear no, ma'am; Tom has only just took it – just took it –'

'Well, Bessie, took it where?'

'Please, ma'am, he took it – took it – took it to keep the frost out of the greenhouse; and please, ma'am, we don't want it, and we're quite hot in bed.'

Dean Hole, A Book About Roses, 1870

The arrival of long-awaited plants is always a pleasure.

If there arrive a flowering-shrub, it is a day of rejoicing with me; or (to use a term in Methodism now so much in fashion) a *Day of Fat Things*. (For you must know, I plant in all seasons.)

William Shenstone, letter to Lady Luxborough,
14 May 1749

Ah, how it cheers the rosarian's heart ... to welcome that package from the nurseries, long and heavy, so cleanly swathed in the new Russian mat, so closely sewn with the thick white cord! His eyes glisten, like the schoolboy's when the hamper comes from home, and hardly, though he has read the story of *Waste not, Want not*, can he keep his knife from the string.

Dean Hole, A Book About Roses, 1870

Showing our plants to visitors is a pleasure too, though discussing them has its problems. One gardener hesitated to inflict Latin names on her guests even when a favourite Olearia gunniana *was quite wrongly identified:*

When my little bush covers itself with white flowers it is often taken for a nice clump of Michaelmas daisies. I don't know what you do when you hear one visitor say to another 'Look at the Michaelmas daisies flowering in June'. If anyone asks me a question I answer it as best I can, but I like people to enjoy the garden in their own way and don't bother them with information and long names unless they want them. I often feel that gardeners can be very tiresome with their long names; in fact I wonder sometimes how ordinary people put up with it. We shouldn't think much of it if doctors peppered their light conversation with all the longest medical terms they could think of.

Margery Fish, *A Flower for Every Day*, 1965

Other gardeners are more resolute:

It is absolutely useless to ask any gardener to spare you Latin names, for the excellent reason that nine out of ten alpine plants haven't got any English name. Even our native alpines are very often as badly off as the newest Himalayan in that respect. They have no names except by the grace of science... At the same time, to be candid, there are some botanical names that are teasers. Where Polish discoverers or Russian explorers come upon the scene the result is apt to be an appalling jangle of horrors. Michaux, Stribnry, Przewalszky, Tchihatchew are responsible for some real jawbreakers; and when it comes to *Michauxia tchihatchewi*, exhausted humanity gives up in despair. However, there is no help for it but to persevere. You cannot talk of these plants by any other name, because they haven't got any other name; so all you can do is to shut your eyes, blow your nose violently three times, and hope that you have sufficiently expressed that you mean *Tchihatchewi*.

Reginald Farrer, *My Rock Garden*, 1907

Imprecise as they are, there is occasionally something to be said in favour of common names, particularly when it comes to night-scented plants:

To give them their botanical names is to divest them of all magic. Reminiscing on frangipani-laden tropical evenings is evocative enough, and circumstances would seldom require the precision of *Plumeria acutifolia*-laden evenings.

Christopher Lloyd, *The Well-Tempered Garden*, 1970

PLEASURES AND PURSUITS

For children the garden has delights unseen by adult eyes. Here young Hatty and Tom explore Hatty's secret territory:

She showed him all her hiding-places: a leafy crevice between a wall and a tree-trunk, where a small human body could just wedge itself; a hollowed-out centre to a box-bush, and a run leading to it...a wigwam shelter made by a re-arrangement of the bean-sticks that Abel had left leaning against the side of the heating-house; a series of hiding-holes behind the fronds of the great ferns that grew along the side of the greenhouse; a feathery tunnel between the asparagus ridges.

Philippa Pearce, *Tom's Midnight Garden*, 1958

The garden's open spaces offer other delights. A popular Victorian pastime appears in literature of the period.

The glory of the Small House at Allington certainly consists in its lawn, which is as smooth, as level, and as much like velvet as grass has ever yet been made to look. Lily Dale, taking pride in her own lawn, has declared often that it is no good attempting to play croquet up at the Great House. The grass, she says, grows in tufts, and nothing that Hopkins, the gardener, can or will do has any effect upon the tufts. But there are no tufts at the Small House. As the squire himself has never been very enthusiastic about croquet, the croquet implements have been moved permanently down to the Small House, and croquet there has become quite an institution...

We may now, I think, go back to our four friends, as they walked out upon the lawn. They were understood to be on a mission to assist Mrs Dale in the picking of peas; but pleasure intervened in the way of business, and the young people, forgetting the labours of their elder, allowed themselves to be carried away by the fascinations of croquet. The iron hoops and the sticks were fixed. The mallets and the balls were lying about; and then the party was so nicely made up! 'I haven't had a game of croquet yet,' said Mr Crosbie. It cannot be said that he had lost much time, seeing that he had only arrived before dinner on the preceding day. And then the mallets were in their hands in a moment.

Anthony Trollope, The Small House at Allington,
1862

The fictional Brackenshaw Park provides a more stately setting for another graceful garden recreation.

The archery-ground was a carefully-kept enclosure on a bit of tableland at the farthest end of the park, protected towards the south-west by tall elms and a thick screen of hollies, which kept the gravel walk and the bit of newly-mown turf where the targets were placed in agreeable afternoon shade. The Archery Hall with an arcade in front showed like a white temple against the greenery on the northern side.

What could make a better background for the flower-groups of ladies, moving and bowing and turning their necks as it would become the leisurely lilies to do if they took to locomotion? The sounds too were very pleasant to hear, even when the military band from Wancester ceased to play; musical laughs in all the registers and a harmony of happy friendly speeches, now rising towards mild excitement, now sinking to an agreeable murmur.

George Eliot, Daniel Deronda, 1876

The real-life joys and tribulations of a sporting afternoon in a Radnorshire garden:

The party at Pont Vaen divided itself into croquet and archery. High tea at 7 just before which someone managed to shoot a chicken with an arrow, or it was said so, and Margaret Oswald told me that as I put my head through the railings to rake a croquet ball out of the field on to the lawn, my head looked so tempting that she felt greatly inclined to shoot at it . . .

After tea Mrs Bridge took us round into the garden

to show us her hives. One bee instantly flew straight at me and stung me between the eyes, as I was poking about the hives in my blind way. I did not say anything about it and Mrs Bridge congratulated me on my narrow escape from being stung. All the while the miserable bee was buzzing about entangled in my beard, having left his sting between my eyes. Consequently I suppose he was in his dying agony. Then we walked round the garden and along the water walk, while the water ran out of my eyes. The pretty waterfall did not show to advantage beneath the bridge for the brook ran very low and humble. Then a wild nonsensical game of croquet in the dark, everyone playing at the same time, and screams of laughter which might be heard almost in the Hay.

Revd Francis Kilvert, Diary, 16 July 1870

In hot weather those of a lazier disposition seek cool retreats:

Summer-houses, good friends, may be regarded as simply useful, as simply ornamental, or as combining both these qualities. Our own peculiar idea about them is that if they are not useful, they are but as stored up firewood, no matter how beautiful in appearance, or how much they may have cost. To begin with the most obvious uses, a summer-house should be adapted for rest, shelter, meditation, conversation, reading, observation, and perhaps conviviality.

Shirley Hibberd, Rustic Adornments for Homes
of Taste, 1856

A poet's summer-house:

I write in a nook that I call my *Boudoir*. It is a summer-house not much bigger than a sedan chair, the door of which opens into the garden, that is now crowded with pinks, roses, and honeysuckles, and the window into my neighbour's orchard ... Having lined it with garden mats, and furnished it with a table and two chairs, here I write all that I write in summer-time, whether to my friends, or to the public. It is secure from all noise, and a refuge from all intrusion; for intruders sometimes trouble me in the winter evenings at Olney. But (thanks to my *Boudoir!*) I can now hide myself from them. A poet's retreat is sacred.

William Cowper, letter to Joseph Hill, 25 June 1785

At Wakes, Selborne, Gilbert White's brother Harry enjoyed appearing in hermit's guise to surprise and entertain visitors.

July 28. – Drank tea 20 of us at the Hermitage: the Miss Batties, and the Mulso family contributed much to our pleasure by their singing, and being dressed as shepherds, and shepherdesses. It was a most elegant evening; and all parties appeared highly satisfied. The Hermit appeared to great advantage.

Gilbert White, *Garden Kalendar*, 1763

It being a very fine moonshine, my wife and Mercer came into the garden, and, my business being done, we sang till about twelve at night, with mighty pleasure to ourselves and neighbours, by their casements opening.

Samuel Pepys, *Diary*, 5 May 1666

It is debatable whether the neighbours were delighted for though Pepys and his maidservant Mercer were musical, Mrs Pepys was tone-deaf.

No garden is complete without seats, but sometimes a head for heights is needed to enjoy them, as at Woburn in Bedfordshire:

there is a seat up in a high tree that ascends from the green fifty steps, that commands the whole park round to see the deer hunted, as also a large prospect of the country...

The Journeys of Celia Fiennes, 1697

For small suburban gardens, where it is not possible to achieve water amphitheatres or even terrace-walks, it will yet be possible to gain a different level in the garden by having recourse to another plan. A flight of wooden, rather ladder-like steps can lead up to a gallery surrounding a portion of the trunk of a tree. This, if the tree chances to be large and overshadowing, will give a very delightful retreat, in which the family can do their reading and writing. There is something that recalls the Swiss Family Robinson about it, and this feeling of a spice of adventure is all the more enjoyable.

Viscountess Wolseley, *Gardens, their Form and Design*, 1919

Sensations of another kind awaited those who sank to rest on the seats in a grotto at Italy's Pratolino palace:

... in this cave on all sides are marble chairs, whereupon passengers willingly sit after their walking: but as soon as they lightly press some of the seats, a pail of water falls upon his head that sits upon it...

Fynes Moryson, *An Itinerary*, 1617

Things were more dignified in the grounds of Pliny's Tuscan villa where he could relax on

a semicircular seat of white marble, shaded by a vine; the vine is supported by four small columns of Carystian marble. From this seat water gushes forth through tiny pipes, just as if it were set in motion by the weight of the persons reclining. It is collected in the hollowed rock, and deposited in a polished marble basin, being so regulated by a hidden contrivance, as to fill it without overflowing it. My picnic tray and the heavier part of my dinner-service are placed on the edge of the basin, the lighter parts make the round of the water, floating in the form of little boats and birds.

> Pliny the Younger, letter to Domitius Apollinaris,
> c. AD 61–113

A more homely Victorian garden retreat:

The south end or corner of a moderate flower garden should be fixed upon for the erection of a root house, which is not an expensive undertaking, and which forms a picturesque as well as a most useful appendage to a lady's parterre. Thinnings of plantations, which are every where procured at a very moderate charge, rudely shaped and nailed into any fancied form, may supply all that is needful to the little inclosure; and a thatch of straw, rushes or heather, will prove a sure defence to the roof and back. There, a lady may display her taste by the beauty of the flowers which she may train through the rural frame-work. There, the moss-rose, the jessamine, the honeysuckle, the convolvulus, and many other bright and beautiful flowers, may escape and cluster around her, as she receives rest and shelter within their graceful lattice-work.

> Louisa Johnson, *Every Lady her own Flower
> Gardener*, 1840

Leafy alcoves and shady walks are the ideal setting for courtship, and for proposals honourable or otherwise.

There was a bower at the further end, with honeysuckle, jessamine, and creeping plants – one of those sweet retreats which humane men erect for the accommodation of spiders.

The spinster aunt took up a large watering-pot which lay in one corner, and was about to leave the arbour. Mr Tupman detained her, and drew her to a seat beside him.

'Miss Wardle!' said he.

The spinster aunt trembled, till some pebbles which had accidentally found their way into the large watering-pot shook like an infant's rattle.

'Miss Wardle,' said Mr Tupman, 'you are an angel.'

'Mr Tupman!' exclaimed Rachael, blushing as red as the watering-pot itself.

'Nay,' said the eloquent Pickwickian – 'I know it but too well.'

'All women are angels, they say,' murmured the lady, playfully.

'Then what can you be; or to what, without presumption, can I compare you?' replied Mr Tupman. 'Where was the woman ever seen who resembled you? Where else could I hope to find so rare a combination of excellence and beauty? Where else could I seek to – Oh!' Here Mr Tupman paused, and pressed the hand which clasped the handle of the happy watering-pot.

The lady turned aside her head. 'Men are such deceivers,' she softly whispered.

'They are, they are,' ejaculated Mr Tupman; 'but not all men. There lives at least one being who can never change – one being who would be content to devote his whole existence to your happiness – who lives but in your eyes – who breathes but in your smiles – who bears the heavy burden of life itself only for you.'

'Could such an individual be found,' said the lady –

'But he *can* be found,' said the ardent Mr Tupman, interposing. 'He *is* found. He is here, Miss Wardle.' And ere the lady was aware of his intention, Mr Tupman had sunk upon his knees at her feet.

'Mr Tupman, rise,' said Rachael.

'Never!' was the valorous reply. 'Oh, Rachael!' – He seized her passive hand, and the watering-pot fell to the ground as he pressed it to his lips. – 'Oh, Rachael! say you love me!'

Charles Dickens, The Pickwick Papers, 1836

John Eames, intent on declaring his love for Lily Dale, meets her in the garden:

'Shall we go into the drawing-room?' she said, feeling that she would be in some degree safer there than out among the shrubs and paths of the garden. And I think she was right in this. A man will talk of love out among the lilacs and roses, who would be stricken dumb by the demure propriety of the four walls of a drawing-room.

Anthony Trollope, The Small House at Allington, 1862

A hopeful suitor declares his love for Daisy Thomas:

... we went out into the garden, her father and I. I said, 'You will be very much surprised but I hope not displeased at what I am going to say to you.' 'What is it?' he said eagerly, 'have you got the living of Glasbury?' 'No, something much nearer to you than that.' 'What is it?' I was silent a minute. I was frightfully nervous. 'I-am-attached-to-one-of-your-daughters,' I said. Just as I made this avowal we came suddenly round the corner upon a gardener cutting a hedge. I feared he had heard my confession, but I was much relieved by being assured that he was deaf. Mr Thomas said I had done quite right in coming to him, though he seemed a good deal taken aback.

He said also a great many complimentary things about my 'honourable high-minded conduct', asked what my prospects were and shook his head over them. He could not allow an engagement under the circumstances, he said, and I must not destroy his daughter's

[98]

peace of mind by speaking to her or showing her in any way that I was attached to her ...

We had been walking along the path between the house and the garden and down the middle garden walk. The place is inextricably entwined in my remembrance with the conversation and the circumstances.

Revd Francis Kilvert, *Diary*, 9 July 1870

Cluny Stanyhurst, 'a fashionable, lean, pale man of thirty-six', walks from his club in eighteenth-century London to the house where he keeps his mistress.

This evening he approached a house in Montagu Square by way of a small walled garden, bisected by a tesselated path, at the back. A trembling copper beech, gay flowers, and the footway of coloured tiles, made this entrance more agreeable than the other, he always thought.

Besides, there was a chance of surprising in an obscure passage Lucy's pert little French maid. The girl was distinctly fetching, with that shy smile of hers combined with a sly look sideways from under the eyelashes. Stanyhurst, going along the path, disturbed a thrush breaking the shell of a snail on the mosaic, and was aware of a swooning, faint scent of stocks. To break a girl among fragrance and colour!

Hugh Edwards, *All Night at Mr Stanyhurst's*, 1933

As we go about our own pursuits in the garden we can enjoy the activities of wildlife and pets.

He is a bad gardener whose garden is kept only for himself. Paradise was not made for Adam only, but for 'every beast of the field and every fowl of the air that was brought unto him' there. And we add largely to the pleasure of our gardens when we look on them not only as pleasant homes for our flowers and fruit, but also as the homes of many lovely and interesting living creatures. We cannot spare the birds, though we may have to pay largely for their beauty and their song. We cannot spare the butterflies and moths, though as caterpillars they are most destructive. I should be sorry not to have the little spider which weaves such a net-work of beauty on our shrubs in the early autumn mornings; and even our greatest enemies, the slugs, snails, and mice, which may be caught and killed without mercy, add to the interest of our garden, and most assuredly, though we may not see it, they have their use.

Canon Ellacombe, *In a Gloucestershire Garden*, 1895

As my garden invites into it all the birds of the country, by offering them the conveniency of springs and shades, solitude and shelter, I do not suffer any one to destroy their nests in the Spring, or drive them from their usual haunts in fruit-time. I value my garden more for being full of blackbirds than cherries, and very frankly give them fruit for their songs.

Joseph Addison, *The Spectator*, 6 September 1712

Sat 28 May 1825. Found the old Frog in my garden that has been there this 4 years I know it by a mark which it recievd from my spade 4 years ago I thought it would die of the wound so I turned it up on a bed of flowers at the end of the garden which is thickly covered with ferns and bluebells I am glad to see it has recoverd in Winter it gets into some straw in a corner of the garden and never ventures out till the beginning of May when it hides among the flowers and keeps its old bed never venturing further up the garden ...

John Clare, *Journal*, 1824-5

October 17. The tortoise not only gets into the sun under the fruit-wall; but he tilts one edge of his shell against the wall, so as to incline his back to its rays: by which contrivance he obtains more heat than if he lay in his natural position. And yet this poor reptile has never read, that planes inclining to the horizon receive more heat from the sun than any other elevation! At four p.m. he retires to bed under the broad foliage of a hollyhock. He has ceased to eat for some time.

Gilbert White, *Naturalist's Journal*, 1782

My great-aunt had a favourite Aberdeen, who, incredible though it may seem, loved ripe gooseberries. He used to sit up, as though he were begging, and eat them and wail aloud every few minutes whenever his nose was pricked.

Eleanour Sinclair Rohde, *The Scented Garden*, 1931

Puss, a pet hare:

I made it my custom to carry him always after breakfast into the garden, where he hid himself generally under the leaves of a cucumber vine, sleeping or chewing the cud till evening; in the leaves also of that vine he found a favourite repast. I had not long habituated him to this taste of liberty, before he began to be impatient for the return of the time when he might enjoy it. He would invite me to the garden by drumming upon my knee, and by a look of such expression as it was not possible to misinterpret. If this rhetoric did not immediately succeed, he would take the skirt of my coat between his teeth, and pull at it with all his force.

William Cowper, *Gentleman's Magazine*, 1784

My garden would not be half the pleasure it is to me without the pussies... They are perfect garden companions. When I am out at work there is sure to be one or other of them close by, lying on my jacket or on a bench if there is one near. When it is Tabby, if there is an empty basket anywhere handy he is certain to get into it... Like most cats he is devoted to the pretty catmint. It is in several places in the garden. He knows where every plant is and never passes one when we are walking together without stopping to nuzzle and nibble it... when he has had his first taste he will push himself right down into the middle of the plant and sometimes lie down and roll in it to get all he can of the sweet smell.

Gertrude Jekyll, *Children and Gardens*, 1908

Another famous cat was commemorated at the Villa Tennyson, San Remo:

Foss is buried in the garden, and I am putting up a little stone memorandum.

Edward Lear, letter to Lord Carlingford, 29 September 1887

Other things too have been buried in gardens: mundane items...

Her mother ripened cream-cheese in the soil, buried deep in their little muslin cloths, the place marked with a stick. Often Susan had been sent to dig them up after the correct two or three days. Once the stick was lost and Dan spent half an hour digging for the missing cheese.

Alison Uttley, *The Country Child*, 1931

... *valuables threatened by the Great Fire of London* ...

Sir W. Batten not knowing how to remove his wine, did dig a pit in the garden, and laid it in there; and I took the opportunity of laying all the papers of my office that I could not otherwise dispose of. And in the evening Sir W. Pen and I did dig another, and put our wine in it; and I my parmazan cheese, as well as my wine and some other things.

Samuel Pepys, Diary, 4 September 1666

... *and even the heart of the gardener himself:*

About two miles from Farnham is More-park, formerly the seat of Sir William Temple, who, by his will, ordered his heart to be put into a china basin, and buried under a sun-dial in his garden, which was accordingly performed.

Daniel Defoe, A Tour Through the Island of Great Britain, 1724 (1748 ed.)

Envoi

A gardener's prayer:

O Lord, grant that in some way it may rain every day, say from about midnight until three o'clock in the morning, but, you see, it must be gentle and warm so that it can soak in; grant that at the same time it would not rain on campion, alyssum, helianthemum, lavender, and the others which you in your infinite wisdom know are drought-loving plants – I will write their names on a bit of paper if you like – and grant that the sun may shine the whole day long, but not everywhere (not, for instance, on spiraea, or on gentian, plantain lily, and rhododendron), and not too much; that there may be plenty of dew and little wind, enough worms, no plant-lice and snails, no mildew, and that once a week thin liquid manure and guano may fall from heaven. Amen.

Karel Čapek, The Gardener's Year, 1929

John Tradescant the Elder – whose collection of curios formed the basis of Oxford's Ashmolean Museum – and his son were gardeners to Charles I and his French wife Henrietta Maria. The following lines appear on their tombstone, which can be found today at the Ashmolean in an obscure corner of the stairway leading to the lavatories.

> Know stranger ere thou pass, beneath this stone
> Lie JOHN TRADESCANT, grandsire, father, son;
> The last dy'd in his spring; the other two
> Liv'd till they had travelled art and nature thru...
> These famous anitiquarians that had been
> Both gardiners to the ROSE and LILLY QUEEN,

ENVOI

Transplanted now themselves, sleep here; and when
Angels shall with their trumpets awaken men,
And fire shall purge the world, these hence shall rise,
And change their garden for a paradise.

> Lines from the Tradescants' tombstone, inscribed
> and erected over their Lambeth grave in 1773

Did you ever meet a gardener, who, however fair his ground, was absolutely content and pleased? ... Is there not always a tree to be felled or a bed to be turfed? Does not somebody's chimney, or somebody's ploughed field, persist in obtruding its ugliness? Is there not ever some grand mistake to be remedied next summer?

> Dean Hole, *A Book About Roses*, 1870

Acknowledgements

My thanks go to the staff at the Bodleian Library, Oxford Central Library, and Burford Branch Library for dealing with many book requests; to the RHS Lindley Library, and Alastair Forsyth of the Royal Commission on Historical Monuments, for their help with several queries; to John Dunbabin, Crispin Gill, and Christopher Hall, who contributed suggestions for this anthology; and especially to my husband Stuart Seager, for his interest, encouragement, and help with research.

The editor and publishers gratefully acknowledge permission to use copyright material in this book:

Sir George Arthur: From *The Letters of Lord and Lady Wolseley* (Heinemann, 1922). By permission of Sir Basil Arthur.

Sir John Betjeman: Originally reproduced from a talk by John Betjeman entitled 'Landscapes with Houses: Kelmscott Manor, Oxfordshire', broadcast on the Home Service, 4 May 1952. By permission of BBC Publications.

Ruth Bidgood: 'Mole-trap', from *The Countryman*, Winter 1968. By permission.

Wilfrid Blunt: In *A Gardener's Dozen* (BBC Publications/Royal Horticultural Society, 1980). Reprinted by permission of BBC Publications.

Ronald Blythe: From *A Book of Gardens* (Cassell, 1963). Reprinted by permission of David Higham Associates Ltd.

E. A. Bowles: From *My Garden in Summer* (T. C. &. E. C. Jack, 1914). Reprinted by permission of Thomas Nelson & Sons Ltd.

Karel Čapek: From *The Gardener's Year*. Reprinted by permission of George Allen & Unwin (Publishers) Ltd.

Michael Dower: Reprinted from *The Countryman*, Summer 1974. By permission.

Hugh Edwards: From *All Night at Mr. Stanyhurst's* (1933). Reprinted by permission of Jonathan Cape Ltd., for the Estate of Hugh Edwards.

Reginald Farrer: From *My Rock Garden* (1907). Reprinted by permission of Edward Arnold (Publishers) Ltd.

Valerie Finnis: In *A Gardener's Dozen* (BBC Publications/Royal Horticultural Society, 1980). Reprinted by permission of BBC Publications.

ACKNOWLEDGEMENTS

Margery Fish: From *A Flower For Every Day*. Reprinted by permission of Faber & Faber Ltd.

Ian Fleming: From *You Only Live Twice* (1964). Reprinted by permission of Jonathan Cape Ltd., for Glidrose Productions Ltd.

H. L. V. Fletcher: From *Purest Pleasure* (Hodder & Stoughton, 1948). Reprinted by permission of Laurence Pollinger Ltd.

Roy Genders: From *Perfume in the Garden* (Museum Press, 1955).

Jason Hill: From *The Contemplative Gardener* (1940). Reprinted by permission of Faber & Faber Ltd.

Susan Hill: From *The Magic Apple Tree* (1982). Reprinted by permission of Hamish Hamilton Ltd. Published in the USA by Holt, Rinehart & Winston, Inc.

Ronald Hingley: From *A New Life of Chekhov*. Copyright © Ronald Hingley 1976. Reprinted by permission of Oxford University Press, and Alfred A. Knopf, Inc.

Revd Francis Kilvert: From *Kilvert's Diary*, ed. William Plomer. Reprinted by permission of Mrs Sheila Hooper and Jonathan Cape Ltd.

Miles Kington: From 'Let's Parler Franglais' column, *Punch*, 19 August 1981. By permission.

Rudyard Kipling: From 'The Glory of the Garden' from *Sixty Poems* (1939) copyright 1911 by Rudyard Kipling. Reprinted by permission of A. P. Watt Ltd., on behalf of The National Trust, and of Doubleday & Company.

Audrey le Lièvre: From *Miss Willmott of Warley Place* (1980). Reprinted by permission of Faber & Faber Ltd.

Christopher Lloyd: From *The Well-Tempered Garden* (1970). Reprinted by permission of Collins Publishers.

Violet Markham: From *Paxton and the Bachelor Duke* (Hodder & Stoughton, 1935). Copyright the Estate of Violet Markham.

C. H. Middleton: From an essay in *The Queen's Book of the Red Cross* (1939). Reprinted by permission of Hodder & Stoughton Ltd.

A. A. Milne: 'Jonathan Jo' from *When We Were Very Young*. Reprinted by permission of Methuen Children's Books, E. P. Dutton, Inc., and McClelland & Stewart, Toronto.

Sir Frederick Moore: From *The Gardener's Chronicle*, 13 March 1937. By permission.

Lady Ottoline Morrell: From *Ottoline, The Early Memoirs of Lady Ottoline Morrell* (1963), ed. Robert Gathorne-Hardy. Reprinted by permission of Faber & Faber Ltd., and Mrs Julian Vinogradoff.

John Nash: In *The Saturday Book*, ed. John Hadfield (Hutchinson, 1957).

Beverley Nichols: From *Down The Garden Path* (Cape, 1932).

ACKNOWLEDGEMENTS

Reprinted by permission of Eric Glass Ltd., as agent for the author.

Philip Oakes: 'Gardening Poem' from *Selected Poems* (Deutsch, 1982). Copyright © 1982 Philip Oakes. Reprinted by permission of Elaine Greene Ltd.

George Orwell: From *Collected Essays, Journalism and Letters*, Vol. 3. Copyright © 1968 by Sonia Brownell Orwell. Reprinted by permission of A. M. Heath & Co. Ltd., for the estate of the late Sonia Brownell Orwell and Martin Secker & Warburg Ltd., and of Harcourt Brace Jovanovich, Inc. First appeared in the *Tribune*, 21 January 1944.

Boris Pasternak: From *Doctor Zhivago*, trans. Max Hayward and Manya Harari. Copyright © 1958 by William Collins Sons & Co. Ltd., and Pantheon Books, Inc. Reprinted by permission of Pantheon Books, a Division of Random House, Inc., and Collins Publishers.

A. Philippa Pearce: From *Tom's Midnight Garden*. Copyright © OUP, 1958. Reprinted by permission of Oxford University Press.

Po-Chü-i: 'I took money and bought flowering trees . . .', from *170 Chinese Poems* (1920), trans. Arthur Waley. Reprinted by permission of Constable Publishers & Alfred A. Knopf, Inc.

Marcel Proust: From *Swann's Way*, translated C. K. Scott Moncrieff and Terence Kilmartin. Translation copyright © 1981 by Random House, Inc., and Chatto & Windus. By permission.

Eleanour Sinclair Rohde: From *The Scented Garden* (1931). Reprinted by courtesy of the Medici Society Ltd., London.

Victoria Sackville-West: From *In Your Garden* (Michael Joseph, 1951). Reprinted by permission of Curtis Brown Ltd., London on behalf of the Estate of Victoria Sackville-West. 'Labour within your garden square' from *The Land* (Heinemann, 1927).

Osbert Sitwell: From *Laughter in the Next Room* (Macmillan, 1949). Reprinted by permission of David Higham Associates Ltd.

D. J. Sutton: 'Lines for a country garden', from *The Countryman*, Summer 1967. By permission.

Graham Stuart Thomas: From *Perennial Garden Plants* (1982). Reprinted by permission of J. M. Dent & Sons Ltd.

R. S. Thomas: 'The Garden' from *The Bread of Truth*. Reprinted by permission of the author and Granada Publishing Ltd.

Flora Thompson: From *Lark Rise to Candleford* (1954). Reprinted by permission of Oxford University Press.

J. R. R. Tolkien: From *Lord of the Rings* (1954). Reprinted by permission of George Allen & Unwin (Publishers) Ltd. Published in the USA by Houghton Mifflin Co.

Anne Treneer: From *Schoolhouse in the Wind* (1944). Reprinted

ACKNOWLEDGEMENTS

by permission of Jonathan Cape Ltd., for the Estate of Anne Treneer.

James Turner: From *A Book of Gardens* (Cassell, 1963). Reprinted by permission of Laurence Pollinger Ltd.

Alison Uttley: From *The Country Child* (1931). Reprinted by permission of Faber & Faber Ltd.

H. G. Wells: From *Mr. Britling Sees It Through* (1916). Reprinted by permission of A. P. Watt Ltd., for the Executors of the Estate of H. G. Wells.

Ralph Wightman: From *A Book of Gardens* (Cassell, 1963). Reprinted by permission of Laurence Pollinger Ltd.

Colin Wilson: From *A Book of Gardens* (Cassell, 1963). Reprinted by permission of Laurence Pollinger Ltd.

P. G. Wodehouse: From *Leave it to Psmith* (Hutchinson Books Ltd., 1923). Reprinted by permission of A. P. Watt Ltd., for Lady Ethel Wodehouse & Hutchinson Group Ltd., and of Scott Meredith Agency, Inc.

Viscountess Wolseley: From *Gardens, Their Form and Design* (1919). Reprinted by permission of Edward Arnold (Publishers) Ltd.

While every effort has been made to secure permission, we may have failed in a few cases to trace the copyright holder. We apologize for any apparent negligence.

The illustrations in this book were taken from the following sources: Reginald Blomfield, *The Formal Garden in England* (London, 1901); *The Gardener's Magazine of Botany*; S. Reynolds Hole, *Our Gardens*, with illustrations by Arthur Rackham (London, 1907) (By courtesy of Mrs Barbara Edwards); Clarence P. Hornung, *Handbook of Early Advertising Art* (New York, 1956); Rose Standish Nichols, *English Pleasure Gardens* (London, 1902); W. Robinson, *The English Flower Garden* (London, 1883).

Index

Addison, J., 30, 44, 76–7, 100
Alcott, Louisa, 27
Armstrong, John, 54–5
Arnim, Countess von, 7–8, 51
Arnold, Matthew, 70–1

Bacon, Francis, 17, 78
Betjeman, John, 84
Bible, 1
Bidgood, Ruth, 64
Blunt, Wilfrid, 74
Blythe, Ronald, 48
Bowles, E. A., 17, 82
Burnett, Frances Hodgson, 20–1, 70
Burney, Fanny, 65–6

Čapek, Karel, 1–2, 49–50, 56–7, 59–60, 104
Chatsworth, Derbyshire, 12
Chekhov, Anton, 4
Clare, John, 36–7, 100–1
Cobbett, William, 9, 17, 44, 51, 86–7
Cowley, Abraham, 25
Cowper, William, 45, 57–8, 63, 87–8, 93–4, 101–2
Crabbe, George, 26
Crisp, Sir Frank, 15

Defoe, Daniel, 103
Dickens, Charles, 19–20, 46, 97–8
Dower, Michael, 5, 55, 68

Earle, Mrs C. W., 5
Edwards, Hugh, 99
Eliot, George, 43, 92
Ellacombe, Canon H., vi, 52–3, 99–100
Evelyn, John, 3, 51, 55, 57, 61, 63, 65

Farrer, Reginald, 17–18, 41–2, 90

Fiennes, Celia, 29–30, 63, 95
Finnis, Valerie, 53
Fish, Margery, 89–90
Fleming, Ian, 39–40
Fletcher, H. L. V., v, 56
Friar Park, Henley, Oxon, 15

Genders, Roy, 79–80
Gerard, John, 69, 71
Gilfillan, Revd George, 35
Godden, Rumer, 31–2
Grahame, Kenneth, 28
Guardian, the, 45
Gumbleton, W. E., 14–15

Hearn, Lafcadio, 40–1
Hibberd, Shirley, 47, 93
Hill, Jason, 23, 75, 76, 85
Hill, Susan, 19, 85
Hingley, Ronald, 4
Hole, S. Reynolds, Dean of Rochester, 15–16, 86, 88–9, 105
Hudson, W. H., 34, 42
Hunt, Leigh, 26–7
Hyll, Thomas, 59, 64, 65, 69, 71

Jefferies, Richard, 53–4
Jekyll, Gertrude, 82, 83, 102
Johns, Captain W. E., 87
Johnson, Louisa, 9, 96

Kilvert, Revd Francis, 36, 65, 82, 92–3, 98–9
Kingsley, Charles, 47–8
Kington, Miles, 22–3
Kipling, Rudyard, 11–12

Lambert, Constant, 16
Lawrence, D. H., 83–4
Lawson, William, 21–2, 64, 77–8
Lear, Edward, 73, 102
Leasowes, The, Shropshire, 35

INDEX

le Lièvre, Audrey, 10–11
Lloyd, Christopher, 83, 90
Loudon, Jane, 56, 82

Mansfield, Katherine, 72–3
Markham, Violet, 12
Middleton, C. H., 51–2
Milne, A. A., 24
Mitford, Mary Russell, 18, 33–4, 58–9
Moore, Sir Frederick, 14–15
Morrell, Lady Ottoline, 15
Moryson, Fynes, 95

Nash, John, 48–9
Nichols, Beverley, 17, 69–70

Oakes, Philip, 61
Orwell, George, 71–2

Parkinson, John, 70, 82
Pasternak, Boris, 84
Paxton, Joseph, 12
Pearce, Philippa, 91
Pepys, Samuel, 3–4, 94–5, 103
Pliny the Younger, 96
Po-Chü-i, 4–5
Pratolino, Italy, 95
Proust, Marcel, 71

Robinson, William, 77
Rohde, Eleanour Sinclair, 10, 101

Sackville-West, Vita, 6–7, 56, 58, 72
Sayes-Court, Kent, 3
Scott, Sir Walter, 34
Shenstone, William, 35, 66, 69, 89

Sissinghurst, Kent, 6–7
Sitwell, Sir George, 16, 38–9
Sitwell, Osbert, 16
Stevenson, Robert Louis, 19
Stockton, Frank R., 66–7
Sutton, D. J., 35

Temple, Sir William, vii, 46, 103
Thomas, Edward, 32–3, 81
Thomas, Graham Stuart, 74
Thomas, R. S., 25
Thompson, Flora, 37–8, 60, 75–6, 84
Tolkien, J. R. R., 33
Tradescant, John, 104–5
Treneer, Anne, 77
Trollope, Anthony, 91–2, 98
Turner, James, 75
Tusser, Thomas, 57

Uttley, Alison, 80, 102

Villa Torlonia, Frascati, 38–9

Waley, Arthur, 4–5
Wells, H. G., 13–14, 27–8
White, Gilbert, 61–2, 63–4, 65, 66, 94, 101
Wightman, Ralph, 23
Wilder, L. B., 80–1
Willmott, Ellen, 10–11
Wilson, Colin, 52
Woburn, Bedfordshire, 63, 95
Wodehouse, P. G., 12–13
Wolseley, Lady, 8
Wolseley, Viscountess Frances, 6, 95
Wordsworth, Dorothy, 60, 62